Adobe®

PHOTOSHOP 6

for PC/MAC

ENI Publishing LTD

5 D Hillgate Place
18-20 Balham Hill
London SW12 9ER

Tel: 020 8673 3366
Fax: 020 8673 2277

e-mail: publishing@ediENI.com
http://www.eni-publishing.com

Straight to the Point collection directed by Corinne HERVO
English edition: Adrienne TOMMY

Foreword

The aim of this book is to let you find rapidly how to perform any task in **Photoshop 6**. Although the examples presented here were conceived under Windows, the same commands can be found on a Macintosh; where shortcut keys differ, the Macintosh equivalent has been given. Some instructions concerning window management, certain dialog boxes such as Save and Open and the use of certain keys do not apply to Photoshop for Macintosh.

The final pages are given over to an **index** of the topics covered.

The typographic conventions used in this book are as follows:

Type faces used for specific purposes:

bold	indicates the option to take in a menu or dialog box.
italic	is used for notes and comments.
Ctrl	represents a key from the keyboard; when two keys appear side by side, they should be pressed simultaneously.

Symbols indicating the content of a paragraph:

▒	an action to carry out (activating an option, clicking with the mouse...).
⇨	a general comment on the command in question.
⤴	a technique which involves the mouse.
⬥	a keyboard technique.
▤	a technique which uses options from the menus.

📖 OVERVIEW

📖 DOCUMENTS

📖 LAYERS AND CHANNELS

📖 SELECTIONS

Adobe Photoshop 6

5 IMAGE MODIFICATION

INDEX

1.1 Overview

A-Starting Photoshop 6

In Windows, click the **Start** button, then drag the pointer up to the **Programs** menu. Point to the **Adobe** menu then the **Photoshop 6.0** menu. Click the **Adobe Photoshop 6.0** option.

On a Macintosh, double-click the shortcut on the desktop.

The first time you start Photoshop, you will be prompted to configure your monitor and the Photoshop colour profile.

⇨ *A shortcut to Photoshop may also exist on the Windows desktop.*

B-Description of the workscreen

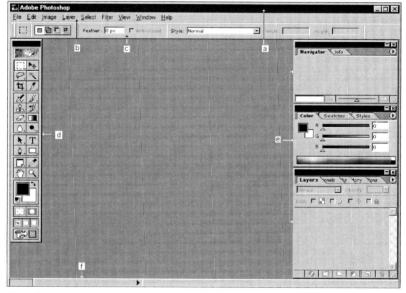

The **title bar** (a).

The **menu bar** (b) contains nine menus.

The **options bar** (c) contains the settings for the currently active tool. The bar's contents change according to the tool. You can hide this bar with the **Windows - Hide Options** command.

The **toolbox** (d) contains your working tools as well as buttons used to control colour and different screen views. Some tools have hidden tools attached to them (this is indicated by a small black triangle at the bottom right of the tool). You can move the toolbox by dragging it by its title bar.

The **floating palettes** (e) give you access to various options. By default, all the palettes are visible, placed in groups of between two and five.

The **status bar** (f) displays information on the zoom level, the size of the active document, the current work status and various other pieces of information. You can hide it with the **Hide Status Bar** option on the **Window** menu.

C-Defining the look of the pointer

▒ **Edit - Preferences - Display & Cursors**

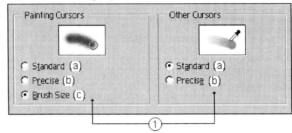

① Define the look of the pointer for the drawing tools and/or for the other tools:

(a)   the pointer takes the form seen on the selected tool's icon.

(b)   the pointer takes the shape of a hair cross or a target.

(c)   the pointer takes the shape defined in the options bar. It indicates the shape and the size of the selected tool.

D-Configuring colour management

▒ **Edit - Color Settings** or Ctrl ⇧ Shift **K** (PC) or ⌘ ⇧ Shift **K** (Mac)

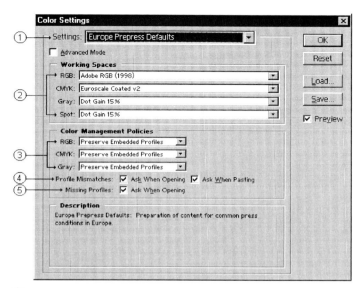

① Select the type of documents you intend to create.

② If you wish, modify the selected default working spaces for that type of document. For an optimal result, do not modify the **RGB** space. For the **CMYK** space, define the ink that will be used according to the paper type. For the **Gray** and **Spot** spaces, give the dot gain (or increase in dot size).

③ Define the colour management policies; for each **RGB**, **CMYK** and **Gray**(scale) space, specify what Photoshop should do when you open an image that has a different colour profile to the one specified in the **Working Spaces** frame:

Off: the open document will have no colour management, and no profile will be used to translate colours.

Preserve Embedded Profiles: the working space used for the document will be the one tagged to it and not the Photoshop space.

Convert to Working RGB: the document's colours are converted in the Photoshop working space.

④ If required, tick the **Ask When Opening** or **Ask When Pasting** option; these display a message when you open or paste (or import) graphics that do not have the stated Photoshop profile so you can choose a different colour management method. If these are deactivated, Photoshop will apply the profile specified under **Color Management Policies** automatically.

⑤ If required, tick this option to display a message when you open graphics that do not have any colour profile specified. If this is deactivated, Photoshop will apply the profile specified under **Color Management Policies** automatically.

1.2 Palettes

A-Looking at the toolbox

If necessary, show the toolbox by activating the **Show Tools** option in the **Window** menu.

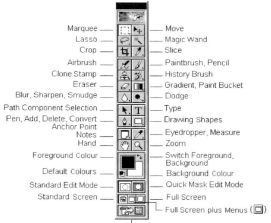

Marquee — Move
Lasso — Magic Wand
Crop — Slice
Airbrush — Paintbrush, Pencil
Clone Stamp — History Brush
Eraser — Gradient, Paint Bucket
Blur, Sharpen, Smudge — Dodge
Path Component Selection — Type
Pen, Add, Delete, Convert Anchor Point — Drawing Shapes
Notes — Eyedropper, Measure
Hand — Zoom
Foreground Colour — Switch Foreground, Background
Default Colours — Background Colour
Standard Edit Mode — Quick Mask Edit Mode
Standard Screen — Full Screen
Full Screen plus Menus (⬜)
Jump to Image Ready

Click a tool's icon to activate it or press the shortcut letter that corresponds to it (if you point to the tool, this letter appears in a ScreenTip). If you want to activate a hidden tool, click and hold the tool button and drag the pointer onto the icon of the required tool.

⇨ *When a tool is active you can adjust its parameters using the options bar.*

⇨ *To restore the default set of tools, click the **Reset All Tools** button in the **Preferences** dialog box (Ctrl **K**).*

B-Working with palettes

Twelve floating palettes are available in Photoshop. Each palette is identified by a tab.

To activate a palette, click the corresponding tab. If the palette you want to use is hidden, activate the corresponding **Show** option in the **Window** menu.

It is possible to separate the palettes by dragging one of the tabs onto the work area. You can regroup them in the same way, by dragging one palette tab onto another.

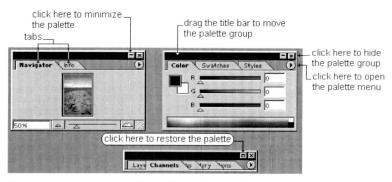

click here to minimize the palette
tabs

drag the title bar to move the palette group

click here to hide the palette group

click here to open the palette menu

click here to restore the palette

⇨ *Some palettes have oblique lines in the bottom right corner: drag this area to resize the palette.*

⇨ *To put the palettes back into their original location, click **Reset Palette Locations** in the **Window** menu.*

⇨ *To restore all the default tool options, click the **Reset All Tools** button in the **Preferences** dialog box ([Ctrl] **K**).*

⇨ *To hide or display all the palettes, press the [⇄] key.*

⇨ *To hide all the palettes in a given group, go to the **Window** menu and choose the **Hide** option that corresponds to the active palette in that group.*

C-Looking at the Info palette

▓ Show the **Info** palette.

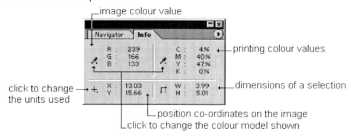

image colour value

printing colour values

click to change the units used

dimensions of a selection

position co-ordinates on the image
click to change the colour model shown

⇨ *When you go on to transform a selection or layer, information relating to printing colours is replaced by the transformation settings: change of scale is indicated by the ⬒ icon and the letters **H** and **W**. The ∠ icon indicates the rotation angle and the ∠⃗ icon indicates the skew angle.*

⇨ *The colour values of the printing colours are by default shown as percentages (%): a ! symbol indicates that the pixel the pointer is on has a non-printing colour.*

⇨ *The pointer's co-ordinates on the image are also indicated. They are displayed in the measurement unit selected in the **Rulers** option, in **Edit - Preferences - Units & Rulers**.*

D-Managing the Swatches palette

Adding/deleting colours in the Swatches palette

▓ Select the foreground colour you want to add to the swatches.

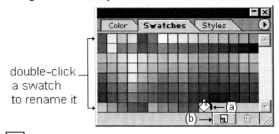

double-click
a swatch
to rename it

▓ Click the button (b) on the **Swatches** palette or click after the last swatch on the palette (a) to add the active foreground colour as a swatch.

▓ Enter the new swatch's **Name** in the text box and click **OK**.

▓ Hold down ⓐShift and click a colour in the swatches to replace it by the new colour.

▓ Hold down Ctrl and click a colour in the swatches to delete that colour.

▓ To return to the default swatches palette, open the palette menu with ⓑ and use the **Reset Swatches** option. Click **OK** on the message that appears.

⇨ *Once you have modified the swatches, you can save the palette with the* **Save Swatches** *option in the* ⓑ *menu. The* **Load Swatches** *option, also in this menu, can be used to activate a previously saved set of swatches.*

⇨ *In the palette menu, there is another option,* **Replace Swatches**. *Unlike the* **Load Swatches** *option which adds a new book to the existing one,* **Replace Swatches** *will erase the current book and replace it with the new one.*

⇨ *The last swatch palette used is saved when you quit Photoshop.*

▓1.3 Viewing

A-Managing the rulers

▓ To show (or hide) the rulers, use the command:
   View - Show Rulers or **Hide Rulers** or Ctrl **R** (PC) or ⓐ⌘ **R** (Mac)

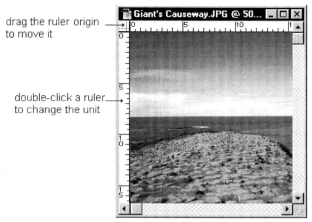

drag the ruler origin to move it

double-click a ruler to change the unit

To take the 0 point back to its default position, double-click the ruler origin square at the intersection of the two rulers.

B-Using guides

Guides are straight lines, visible on the screen but non-printing. They make it easier to position and align elements within the image.

If the rulers are not visible, display them (**View - Show Rulers**).

Point to either the vertical or horizontal ruler depending on what sort of guide you want to create and drag the dotted line onto the image until you have placed the guide in the required position.

⇨ *By default, when you move elements close to the guides, they snap (or are attracted to) the guides. To stop this, deactivate the **View - Snap To - Guides** option. The document's edges are also "magnetic"; to deactivate snapping on them, use **View - Snap To - Document Bounds**.*

Select the ▶+ tool, point to the guide you want to move and drag the guide into its new position.

To delete a guide, drag it out of the image area or onto the rulers. To delete all the guides, use the **Clear Guides** option in the **View** menu.

⇨ *To lock the guides into position, activate the **View - Lock Guides** option or* Ctrl Alt *;.*

⇨ *To define the appearance of the guides, use the **Preferences (Edit - Preferences - Guides & Grid)** or double-click a guide with the ▶+ tool.*

C-Using the grid

Like guides, the grid helps you to place and organise elements on an image: it also attracts objects.

To show or hide the grid, use:

View
Show
Grid

 ' (PC)
' (Mac)

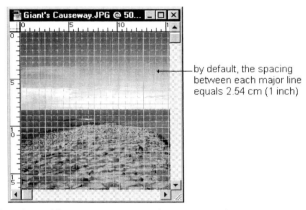

by default, the spacing between each major line equals 2.54 cm (1 inch)

To define the grid parameters, use the command:
Edit - Preferences - Guides & Grid

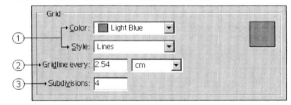

① Define the colour and style for the major grid.

② Indicate how far apart to space the major lines.

③ Specify the number of subdivisions between each major one.

⇨ *To deactivate snapping, use the command **View - Snap To - Grid**.*

D-Using the Measure tool

Click the **Measure** ⬚ tool button (which may be hidden by the **Eye-dropper** ⬚) and point to the place on the image where you want to take a measurement.

Drag to make the measurement. Hold down ⬚Shift while you drag if you want to measure on a horizontal, vertical or 45° angle.

*The measurement is displayed in the **Info** palette and on the options bar.*

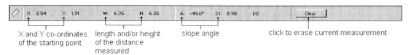

X and Y co-ordinates of the starting point   length and/or height of the distance measured   slope angle   click to erase current measurement

▨ To modify the measure, drag one of its ends. To move it without changing its length, drag the measuring segment.

▨ To measure a specific angle or make two measurements simultaneously, press down  (⌐ on Mac) and drag from one of the ends to draw a second measuring line.

E-Changing the zoom

🖰▨ Click the 🔍 tool button.

▨ Click the part of the image you wish to zoom in on or drag a selection marquee (a dotted rectangle) around it to limit what is seen to just that part.

The zoom value is indicated on the window's title bar.

▨ To reduce the zoom, make sure the 🔍 tool is active, hold down `Alt` (⌐) and click.

▨ To take the image back to a 100% zoom level, double-click the 🔍 tool button.

⇨ *When the image is larger than the window, you can use the scroll cursors or the ✋ tool to scroll the window's contents.*

⇨ *To define a precise zoom, type a value in the first box on the status bar and enter.*

⇨ *To resize the document window automatically to suit the zoom level, tick the **Resize Windows to Fit** option on the options bar with the 🔍 tool active.*

📦▨ Use one of these shortcuts:

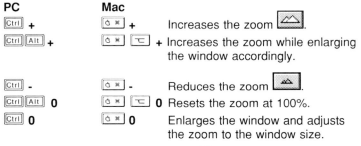

PC   **Mac**

`Ctrl` +   `⇧ ⌘` +   Increases the zoom 🔺.

`Ctrl` `Alt` +   `⇧ ⌘` `⌐` + Increases the zoom while enlarging the window accordingly.

`Ctrl` -   `⇧ ⌘` -   Reduces the zoom 🔻.

`Ctrl` `Alt` 0   `⇧ ⌘` `⌐` 0 Resets the zoom at 100%.

`Ctrl` 0   `⇧ ⌘` 0   Enlarges the window and adjusts the zoom to the window size.

⇨ *You can also use the options in the **View** menu.*

⇨ *To display the image window over the entire work area, while keeping the menu bar, click the ▢ button at the base of the toolbox. To obtain a larger displaying surface, click the ▢ button. To return to a standard screen mode, click the ▣ button.*

F-Modifying the size of the canvas

▨ If necessary, choose a background colour to fill the new areas of the document. This is not useful if your image contains only layers and no **Background**.

▨ **Image - Canvas Size**

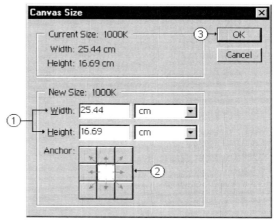

① Determine the new width and height of your document, specifying the desired unit of measurement.

② Specify the image position by clicking one of the nine buttons.

③ Click to confirm.

⇨ *If the values you give are smaller than the actual image size, Photoshop will offer to crop the image, by removing the parts surrounding the image, in accordance with the image position you specified using the **Anchor** buttons.*

G-Using the Navigator palette

If necessary, show the **Navigator** palette.

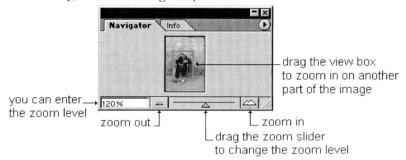

you can enter the zoom level

drag the view box to zoom in on another part of the image

zoom out ⌐

zoom in

drag the zoom slider to change the zoom level

➪ *You can also hold down* ⌐Ctrl⌐ *(PC) or* ⌐⌘⌐ *(Mac) and drag a marquee (an invisible rectangle) around the area you wish to zoom.*

➪ *To change the colour of the view box, open the **Navigator** palette menu (⊙), click **Palette Options**, select a **Color** and click **OK**.*

H-Using several views on an image

Open the document of your choice.

View - New View

A new window for this document is displayed.

➪ *A new view does not create a new document. If you change the image on one view, all the other views are altered in turn.*

2.1 Documents

A-Opening a document

- **File - Open** or ⌐Ctrl⌐ **O** (PC) or ⌐⇧ ⌘⌐ **O** (Mac)

- Using the **Look in** list, go to the folder containing the file you want to open. Double-click each folder icon to see its contents.

- Select the name of the file you want to open and click the **Open** button.

- If the image does not have a colour profile or if it is different to the one used in the working space, a warning message may ask you how to manage colour display (cf. Configuring colour management):

In this example, the colour profile used is different to the one used in the working space. Depending on your needs, keep the profile or convert it, but avoid deleting it.

You may, at this point, see another message informing you that the image has no color profile tagged to it. For good colour results, you should assign a profile (generally the default RGB working profile).

- Activate the required option and click **OK**.

⇨ *The **Open As** option in the **File** menu enables you to open images of unknown type (for example, files with the wrong extension). You can see all the files in the dialog box, so proceed as if opening a normal document and give the file type in the **Open As** box.*

⇨ *You can access recently used documents with the **Open Recent** option in the **File** menu: this saves the names of the last four documents used.*

B-Saving a document in a specific format

Defining a saving format

File - **Save As** or `Ctrl` `⇧ Shift` **S** (PC) or `⌘` `⇧ Shift` **S** (Mac)

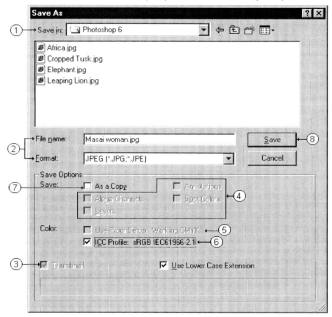

① Go to the folder in which you want to save the file.

② Enter the document name and select the saving format.

③ Tick this option to save a thumbnail of the picture in the Windows Explorer. This option will only be available if you modify the file saving options in **Edit - Preferences - Saving Files**.

④ If necessary indicate whether or not these elements should be saved with the document (if you deactivate the **Layers** option, the image will be flattened during the save).

⑤ If necessary, tick this option to convert your document automatically to the colour space defined in the colour profile management settings.

⑥ Tick this option to memorise the colour profile defined in Photoshop.

⑦ Tick this option to make a copy of the current document.

⑧ Click to save the document.

Depending on the format selected, a second dialog box opens so that you can set the specific saving parameters for the chosen format. Look through the subheadings below for details on the various file formats you can use.

JPEG format

This format is often used for images made for publishing on the Internet or for multimedia applications. It has the advantage of considerably reducing the document size.

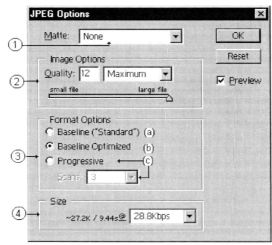

① Choose the colour used for the image background, that is for the transparent areas.

② Set the required quality for the image. This can vary from 0 (**Low** quality) to 12 (**Maximum** quality). The lower the quality, the more the image is compressed and vice versa.

③ Select one of the JPEG format options:

(a) this is the traditional format.

(b) this format optimises the image's colour quality and creates a smaller document.

(c) the image is displayed in **3** to **5 Scans**. As it is downloaded, the image appears gradually, in a more and more detailed form.

④ Choose a size if you want the size of the document to appear along with the speed at which it can be downloaded, depending on the modem speed. This is just an indication.

Photoshop EPS format

This format is used by most desktop publishing (DTP) applications. In Photoshop, this format can save duotones and drawing objects. On the other hand, it cannot save alpha channels or spot colours.

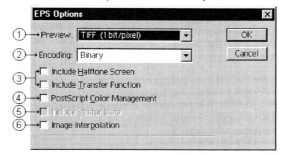

① Select a preview option:

None
No preview is saved and the image will not have any preview when integrated into a DTP application.

TIFF (1 bit/pixel)
In the DTP application the document preview will be in black and white but the image will be printed in colour.

TIFF (8 bits/pixel)
The image will be previewed in colour. The document will be much larger.

② Specify the encoding option that will be used during printing:

ASCII
This is the basic encoding. Use it if you experience printing errors or difficulties.

Binary
This is generally the encoding used for separating films before sending them to a print shop.

JPEG
This is the fastest type of encoding but printing quality is subsequently impaired.

③ Tick these options to save these two settings with the document.

④ Tick this option if you are printing on a PostScript printer and you have not converted the picture to the printer's colour model. If your image is in CMYK, you can only activate this option if you have a level 3 PostScript printer. For level 2 PostScript printers, convert to Lab before saving the document.

⑤ Tick this option to keep vectorial data (such as drawn paths) in the document.

⑥ Tick this option to improve the printed result from a low-resolution image.

PDF format

This format is more universal than the others. It can be read by a PC, a UNIX workstation or a Macintosh without any problems. It is an electronic publishing format which can save not only photographic images but also vector graphics, text, video, sound and can also create hyperlinks. Of course in Photoshop, this is limited to images. This format saves paths, so you can create transparent areas but does not save Alpha channels or spot colours.

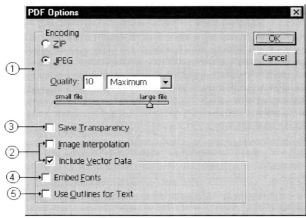

① Select the type of encoding: **ZIP** encoding compresses the image without loss of colour information and **JPEG** encoding compresses the image according to the JPEG format, so with some loss of information. You should specify a **Quality** as with the standard JPEG format.

② Define these options as for EPS format.

③ Tick this option to preserve transparent areas when you import this document into another application.

④ Tick this option if you want the document to display and print correctly, no matter what computer you use to view it.

⑤ Tick this option to replace the text with vectorial information. This reduces the document size but means you can no longer search for text with a PDF viewer such as Acrobat Reader.

BMP format

This is the traditional Windows format. It saves images in RGB, grayscale and indexed color. It cannot save Alpha channels, spot colours or drawn paths.

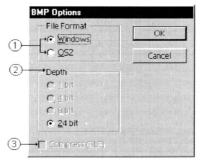

① Activate the **OS2** option if the image is to be exported to a computer equipped with an OS/2 system, otherwise, leave **Windows** active.

② Select the colour resolution.

③ For images in grayscale or indexed color (8 bits maximum), you can activate this option to reduce the document size (this compression does not lose any information but some applications cannot manage it).

TIFF format

This format is primarily used for images that will be printed directly from Photoshop or after integration in a desktop publishing application such as XPress. This format does not suffer any colour information loss and can save Alpha channels and spot colours but cannot manage multichannel images, duotones and drawn paths. It also offers good image compression. It also ensures easy exchanges between PC and Macintosh systems.

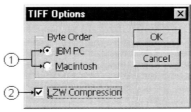

① Select the format according to the type of computer you are using to work on the image.

② Tick this option to reduce the file size. Compressed images take longer to open and save, as the image has to be compressed or decompressed.

⮫ *Most applications, but not all, manage **LZW Compression**.*

DOCUMENTS

C-Other formats recognised by Photoshop

When opening or saving a document, select one of the following formats:

Amiga IFF (*.JFF): this is the standard format for Amiga computers. It is also used for Deluxe Paint on a PC. This format cannot manage CMYK images, alpha channels, spot colours or drawn paths.

CompuServe GIF: this is a frequently used format for online display or for multimedia applications. This format has a high compression capacity without information loss.

EPS TIFF or EPS PICT Preview: this format can only be used to open documents. It allows you to open documents whose format is not supported by Photoshop but which contain low-resolution preview files.

Filmstrip (*.FLM): this format is used to open film files from the Adobe Premiere video editing application. You can only use this format to save existing Filmstrip documents.

FlashPix (*.FPX): this format was designed to speed up the transfer of large, high-resolution files in applications supporting the FlashPix technology. This format manages RGB and grayscale models. It cannot save Alpha channels or spot colours or drawn paths.

Kodak Photo CD (*.PCD): this format lets you open images from a Kodak Photo CD disk. You cannot save a file in this format.

PCX (*.PCX): this format is often recognised by PC applications. It manages RGB, grayscale, indexed color and bitmap images. It does not save alpha channels or spot colours or drawn paths.

Photoshop DCS 1.0 & 2.0: the DCS 2.0 format allows you to save multichannel images for specific printing work as well as spot channels and an alpha channel. The DCS 1.0 format is equivalent to the EPS format except it creates five files instead of just one for the EPS format.

PICT Resource (*.PCT;*.PIC): this is a format from the Macintosh environment. It can memorise photographic images and also vector graphics. This format only manages RGB, indexed color or grayscale images and does not save drawn items.

Pixar (*.PXR): this format was designed to exchange images with PIXAR workstations, which use high-end 3D graphics programmes.

PNG (*.PNG): this format is used to publish images on the Internet. It can save an Alpha channel with images in RGB or grayscale to obtain a result similar to a GIF89a format but in millions of colours. It saves no Alpha channel with Bitmap or indexed color images. Some Web browsers do not recognise this format. Select an **Adam7** interlace if you want the image to appear gradually during downloading. To optimise compression, select a **Filter**. Opt for **None** for Bitmap or indexed color images. You can also choose another filter for other image modes. An **Adaptive** filter selects the most appropriate filter for the image from the various ones on offer.

18

Raw (*.RAW): this is an image format which allows you to transfer files to other systems or specific applications. It can save alpha channels on RGB, CMYK and grayscale images. Other modes are supported (except Bitmap) but the alpha channels are not saved. Drawn paths are not saved either. Be careful, the size and color mode of an image are not saved, so you should note them for any future opening.

Scitex CT (*.SCT): this format is used to process high-end images on Scitex systems. It manages RGB, CMYK and grayscale images. It does not save Alpha channels or spot colours or drawn paths. It often creates very large files. Scitex systems produce few moiré patterns and are often used for professional colour prints.

Targa (*.TGA; *.VDA; *.ICB; *.VST): this format is recognised by many PC applications. It supports RGB 32 Bit modes with an alpha channel and RGB 16 and 24 Bit modes without alpha channels.

⇨ *With some formats, you may be able to set extra options before saving.*

D-Saving an image for use on the Web

▓ **File - Save for Web** or `Ctrl` `Alt` `⇧ Shift` **S** (PC) or `⌘ ⌥` `⌐` `⇧ Shift` **S** (Mac)

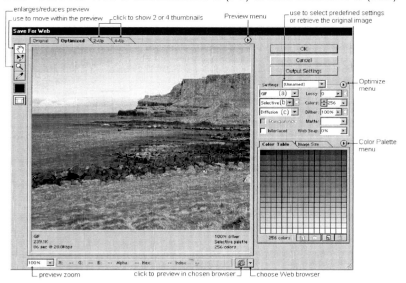

Defining colour conversion options for GIF or PNG-8 formats

▓ Select the **Saving format (a)** that you wish to use.

▓ Change the settings for the conversion to indexed color. See chapter 5.5 - D - Converting an RGB image into Indexed Color, for further details.

Dialog box option	Corresponding option in the indexed color conversion dialog box
Color reduction algorithm (b)	Palette
Colors	Colors
Transparency	Transparency
Matte	Matte
Dithering algorithm (c)	Dither
Dither	Amount

▨ To improve the color conversion result on a specific area of the image, click the [≡] button next to the **Color reduction algorithm option** (b). This zone must have been defined previously with a saved selection, if no selection has been saved, this button is unavailable.

▨ Define the dithering on a specific area of the image by clicking the [≡] button next to the **Dither** option. This zone must have been defined previously with a saved selection, if no selection has been saved, this button is unavailable. In this case, or if you do not wish to improve the outcome of any area, go directly to defining the loss of quality (**Lossy** - see the following point).

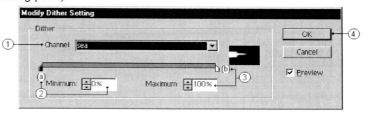

① Select the saved channel whose dithering you wish to optimise.

② Drag the cursor (a) or enter a value to define the dithering on the areas outside the saved selection.

③ Drag the cursor (b) or enter a value to define the dithering on the selected area.

④ Click to confirm.

▨ If you selected **GIF** format, determine how **Lossy** the conversion can be (how much the quality can be reduced). This allows the GIF format to drop a certain amount of colour information, as JPEG format can, which aims to reduce the file size. Generally, a value of between 5 and 10 will not affect the quality. This option is not available if you ticked the **Interlace** or if you chose **Pattern** or **Noise** dithering (c).

▨ You can limit quality loss on an area of the image by clicking the [≡] button next to the **Lossy** option (for **GIF** format). This zone must have been defined previously with a saved selection, if no selection has been saved, this button is unavailable.

- As with dithering optimisation, select the saved **Channel** whose "lossiness" you wish to control, then use the **Maximum** and **Minimum** options and cursors to set the quality loss.
- Click **OK**.
- Set the **Web Snap** option on the colour palette. The higher the value given, the more Web-safe the colours used for the conversion (meaning they can be managed with the 256-colour palette used by Web browsers).

  If you leave a value less than 100%, you can see a preview of the image as it will appear in 256 colours by activating the **Browser Dither** option in the **Preview** menu (⏵).

- Activate the 🖉 tool in the dialog box if you wish to apply one of these effects:

  - Force a colour from the **Original** image into the **Color Table**. To do this, click the **Original** tab at the top of the dialog box, then click the desired colour an return to the **Optimized** image by clicking that tab. The colour is saved but for now it has not been applied to the palette (see next point).

  - Define a colour from the image as the **Matte** colour: to do this, click a colour in the image and select **Eyedropper Color** in the drop-down list on the **Matte** option.

- If necessary, redefine one or more colours from the **Color Table**. To do this, double-click a colour in the palette or use one of the following options:

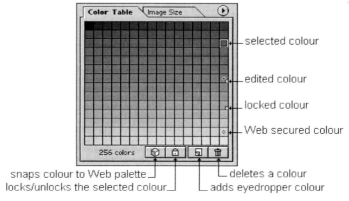

⇨ *The **Save** and **Sort** commands from the **Color Table** palette menu can help you to customise the color table.*

*You can use the **Save Color Table** or **Load Color Table** options in the **Color Table** palette menu to save and re-use specific tables.*

Setting JPEG optimisation options

- Select **JPEG** as the **Optimized file format (a)**.

- Set the required **Compression quality (b)**, from a **Low** quality, of **0** to a **Maximum** quality of **100**. The lower the quality chosen, the more the image will be compressed and vice versa.

- Define the quality for a specific area of the image by clicking the ▣ button next to the **Quality** option. This zone must have been defined previously with a saved selection, if no selection has been saved, this button is unavailable.

- Select the saved **Channel** then drag the cursor ◢ or enter a value in the **Minimum** option to define the quality of the areas outside the saved selection and drag the cursor ◿ or enter a value in the **Maximum** option to define the quality of the selected area. Click **OK**.

- Tick the **Optimized** option to improve the image's colour quality and create a smaller file.

- Tick the **ICC Profile** option to keep this profile with the image. This enables certain browsers to use the ICC profile to work with the image's colour space and ensure good colour correction. Keeping the profile increases the file size.

- Set the amount of **Blur** that will be applied to the image. This option applies a gaussian blur to the image to eliminate stray pixels. This value can vary from **0** to **2** but the blur may be excessive if you go over **0.5**.

- Select the **Matte** colour to be used to fill transparent areas. This option is only useful if your picture does not contain a **Background** layer. In general, set the colour used as the background of the HTML page in which you are integrating the picture.

Setting PNG-24 transparency options

- Select **PNG-24** as the **Optimized file format (a)**.

- Tick the **Transparency** option to preserve the image's transparent areas. This option will only be available if the image has a **Background** layer. This option is useful if you are integrating the picture into an HTML page with a patterned background.

- Select the **Matte** colour to be used to fill transparent areas. This option is only useful if your picture does not contain a **Background** layer and if you are not using the **Transparency** option. In general, set the colour used as the background of the HTML page in which you are integrating the picture.

Setting options common to all formats

▨ Tick the **Progressive** option (for JPEG format) or the **Interlace** option (for other formats) if you wish the image to display gradually during downloading. This creates a slightly larger file.

▨ If you wish, modify the **Image Size** with the options found under the **Image Size** tab, next to the **Color Table** tab. To set these options, refer to the Image Modification section, Images chapter, "Changing an image's size and/or resolution"; the **Quality** option corresponds to the **Resample Image** option.

▨ Click the **Apply** button if you have resized the image.

▨ If necessary, you can define the slice options, by activating the ⬚ tool on the dialog box then double-clicking a slice defined on the image.

⇨ You can also ask Photoshop to set the save options appropriate to the file size, by using the *Optimize to File Size* command in the *Optimize* menu (click the ⬚ button to the right of the *Settings* box). Give the *Desired File Size* (in Kb) and click *OK*.

⇨ You can use the *Save Settings* command in the *Optimize* menu to save the settings, so you can apply them to other pictures. They will subsequently be available in the *Settings* list box.

⇨ You can hide or display slices by clicking the ⬚ button on the *Save For Web* dialog box.

Saving the image

▨ Check the image quality using one of the following commands in the **Preview** menu:

Uncompensated Color: to see the image without any colour adjustment (which amouts to not checking at all).

Standard Windows Color: to view the image as under Windows.

Standard Macintosh Color: to view the image as on a Macintosh.

Use Document Color Profile: to view the image using its ICC profile.

▨ Check how quickly the image will download by selecting a **Download Rate** in the **Preview** menu.

▨ If necessary, click the button representing the selected browser (at the bottom of the dialog box) to view the image in that browser. Close the browser window to return to Photoshop.

▨ Activate the thumbnail that corresponds to the format in which you want to save the image.

▨ Click **OK**.

▨ Go to the folder into which you wish to save and enter the **File name** for the document.

- Select what you wish to save in the **Save as type** list:

  HTML and Images: to create an HTML page containing the picture, automatically. The image(s) generated (if you have created slices) will be saved in the **Images** folder created within the selected folder, while the HTML page will be saved directly in the selected folder.

  Images Only: to save only the image(s) you have generated.

  HTML Only: to save only the HTML page with its references to the image but not the image itself.

- If you select **HTML Only** or **HTML and Images** as the **Save as type** option and you have not already set the **Output Settings** in the **Save For Web** dialog box, click the **Output Settings** button to define them now.

- If your image includes slices, select the slices you want to save. You can save **All Slices** or just the **Selected Slices** that you chose in the **Save For Web** dialog box.

- Click the **Save** button.

⇨ *To optimise an image for the internet, especially to animate it, or to create an image map or other web effects, you can transfer the picture to Image-Ready. To do this, save the picture then click the* *button at the bottom of the toolbox.*

⇨ *To add copyright protection to your image, use the **Embed Watermark** command (**Filter - Digimarc - Embed Watermark**). You will have to register yourself with the Digimarc Corporation to obtain a creator ID.*

E-Creating a Web photo gallery

You can create a photo gallery and publish it on the Internet.

- Close the documents you wish to include in the gallery.

- **File - Automate - Web Photo Gallery**

24

Defining the general Web gallery settings

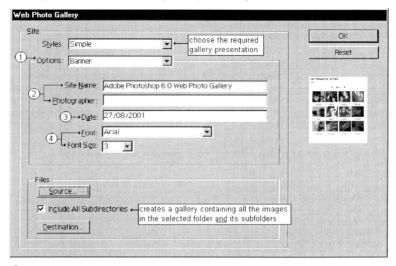

① Select **Banner**.

② Enter the name of the site you are creating then the photographer's name in the appropriate boxes.

③ Enter the date that should appear on the Web site.

④ Select the font and font size used to display the banner's information. The **Font Size** is not in points but corresponds to the **SIZE** attribute used by the <**FONT**> tag in the HTML page:

SIZE=	1	2	3	4	5	6	7
Size in points	9	10	12	14	18	24	36

Defining the options for the Web gallery images

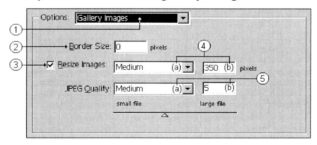

① Select the **Gallery Images** option.

② Define the width of the frame that surrounds the image. If you enter **0**, no frame will be created.

③ Tick this option if you wish to publish the images in the gallery smaller than their original size. If you wish to leave the images at their original size, you should only activate this option if you want to change the image quality.

④ To set the size of the images in the gallery, select a size (a) or enter a value (b).

⑤ Select a **JPEG Quality** (a) for when the images in the gallery are saved in **JPEG** format or enter a value (b) between **0** (**Low** quality) and **12** (**Maximum** quality).

Defining the options for the Web gallery thumbnails

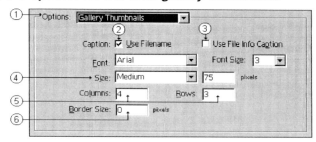

① Select **Gallery Thumbnails**.

② Tick this option if you want the image name to appear beneath its thumbnail in the home page.

③ Tick this option if you want the image's caption to appear beneath its thumbnail.

④ Select the size of the thumbnails that will appear in the gallery home page.

⑤ Choose how many **Columns** or **Rows** should be used to display the thumbnails in the home page. The number of thumbnails that can be shown on one page without having to use the scroll bars can vary, depending on the thumbnail size and the screen resolution used.

⑥ Define the width of the frame around the image. If you enter **0**, no frame will be created.

Defining the Web gallery colour options

▨ Select **Custom Colors** in the **Options** list.

▨ Click the swatch that corresponds to the gallery element whose colour you want to change. If you used the **Border Size** option to define a frame for the images and/or thumbnails, this frame will take on the colour of the **Link**, **Active Link** or **Visited Link** accordingly.

Creating the Web gallery

▨ Click the **Source** button in the **Files** frame to specify which folder contains the images you want to use for the Web gallery.

▨ Select the folder concerned and click **OK**.

░ Click the **Destination** button in the **Files** frame then select the folder in which the Web gallery will be stored. This folder must be different from the **Source** containing the originals.

░ Click **OK** to create the gallery.

The images are resampled then placed in subfolders within the destination folder. Once the gallery has been created, Photoshop displays it in the default Web browser.

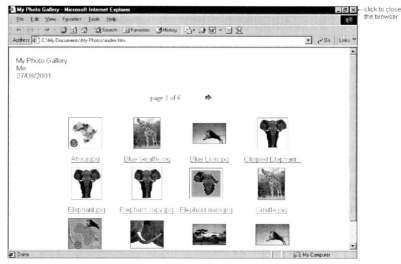

░ Click the ◄ or ► arrow to show the previous or next page of the home page.

░ Click an image or its name to see it full size.

░ To redisplay the gallery at a later time, double-click the **Index.htm** file located in the destination folder.

➪ *The only way to update a gallery, if you have deleted images from the folder, or added new ones, is to create the gallery all over again.*

➪ *Multichannel images often suffer significant colour degradation as they are converted to RGB mode before being displayed in the gallery.*

➪ *EPS or DCS images including a clipping mask will appear as a whole image, without being clipped.*

➪ *GIF89a and PNG images with transparent backgrounds will appear as whole images, the transparent background filled with a single colour.*

➪ *To customise your gallery, modify the HTML pages generated by Photoshop.*

F- Creating a new document

File - New or ⌈Ctrl⌉ N (PC) or ⌈⌥ ⌘⌋ N (Mac)

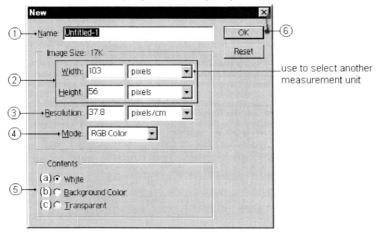

① If you wish, enter the name of the new document.

② Enter the document size.

③ Define the image resolution: the 72 ppi resolution corresponds to the resolution of the monitor and is suitable for images destined to stay on screens. For images made for printing, you should choose a resolution between 150 and 600 ppi depending on the quality required.

④ Select the image's colour mode.

⑤ Define the background, choosing between:

(a) to make the background white.

(b) to use the active background colour.

(c) to make the background a transparent layer. This transparent "colour" is shown on the screen as a grey and white chessboard.

⑥ Click to create the new document.

⇨ *It is possible to define the settings of the transparent colour. To do this, choose **Edit - Preferences - Transparent & Gamut**.*

⇨ *You can use the **File - File Info** command to define information about the document.*

G-Creating a contact sheet

When a folder contains a certain number of images, you may like to create a catalogue of miniature prints called a contact sheet.

Close the documents that you want to include in the contact sheet.

File - Automate - Contact Sheet II

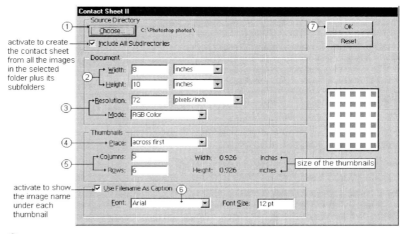

① Select the folder containing the images you wish to display on your contact sheet.

② Define the dimensions of the contact sheet.

③ Choose the resolution and a colour mode.

④ Select whether you want to read the contact sheet in rows or columns.

⑤ Determine the number of columns and rows that you wish to appear.

⑥ Define the font used for the image's legend.

⑦ Click to make the contact sheet.

The images are resampled then placed on a new document with a single layer for all the thumbnails.

⇨ *You cannot update a contact sheet. When images are removed from or added to the folder, you simply make a new contact sheet.*

H-Creating a picture package

As well as creating a catalogue in the form of a contact sheet and a photo gallery, you can also duplicate an image in different formats on the same page. This picture package is based on a similar practice used by professional photo studios.

▓ **File - Automate - Picture Package**

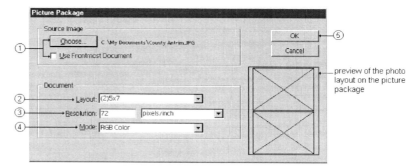

preview of the photo layout on the picture package

① Select the image that will be used in the picture package or, if the image is already open in Photoshop, activate the **Use Frontmost Document** option.

② Select the image layout you wish to use for the picture package.

③ Define the resolution for the picture package.

④ Select the colour mode for the picture package. As a picture package is generally made to be printed, the most frequently used modes are **Grayscale** and **CMYK Color**. If the source image is in another mode such as **RGB Color** or **Lab Color**, it would be preferable to prepare the images before making your picture package.

⑤ Click to create the picture package.

I- Opening an Illustrator document

▨ **File - Open** or ⌨ Ctrl **O** (PC) or ⌨ ⇧ ⌘ **O** (Mac)

▨ Select the Illustrator document you wish to open then click **Open**.

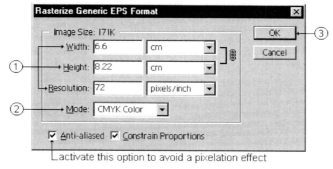

activate this option to avoid a pixelation effect

① Depending on your needs, adjust the settings to obtain the width, height and resolution that you require.

② Select the colour mode that should be used.

③ Click to open the document.

*If Photoshop cannot correctly retrieve some of the character fonts, it may display a message, asking if you wish to **Continue** or **Cancel** opening the Illustrator file. This font problem usually produces no real problems on the outcome.*

As a rule, if an error message of this type appears, click **Continue**, if only to check the result.

The Illustrator drawing is placed on a layer in a new Photoshop document. You can now apply all the Photoshop retouch and transformation features.

⇨ *To import an Illustrator drawing into an existing Photoshop document, use the **File - Place** command.*

⇨ *You can also import an image or a drawing from an Acrobat (.pdf) document.*

J- Exporting paths to Illustrator

▓ **File - Export - Paths to Illustrator**

① Select the folder in which you wish to save the paths.

② Select the path you wish to export: the **Document Bounds** option lets you retrieve in Illustrator the crop marks corresponding to the size of the image but does not let you retrieve the paths.

③ Enter the name of the document that will contain the paths.

④ Click to export the path.

⇨ *When you open the document in Illustrator or another vector graphics application, the paths will be invisible because they are exported without any fill or stroke colour.*

K-Converting an Acrobat document to a Photoshop image

First method

▓ File - Automate - Multi-Page PDF to PSD

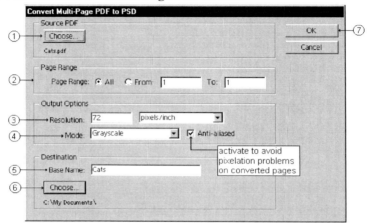

① Select which Acrobat document is to be converted.

② Specify which pages of the Acrobat document you wish to convert.

③ Select the output resolution you wish to obtain after converting the Acrobat document (which is a PostScript document).

④ Select the colour mode for the image.

⑤ If necessary, select a base name for the created documents.

⑥ Choose in which folder the converted images will be placed.

⑦ Click to convert.

*Each page of the Acrobat document is converted from a vector graphic to a Photoshop image then saved in the destination folder. It will be called **Base Name 0001** for the first page, **Base Name 0002** for the second page and so on.*

Second method

▓ File - Import - PDF Image

▓ Select the PDF document you wish to import and click the **Open** button.

▓ Select the image from the Acrobat document that you want to import, using the navigation buttons or the **Go to image** button.

This step is not necessary if you want to import all the images from the PDF file.

▓ Click **OK** to import the selected image or the **Import all images** button to import all the images within the PDF document.

⇨ *You can also import the annotations from an Acrobat document with the File - Import - Annotations command.*

▓▓2.2 Printing

A-Printing an image

▓ **File - Print** or Ctrl **P** (PC) or ⌘ **P** (Mac)

▓ If required, select the part of the image you wish to print.

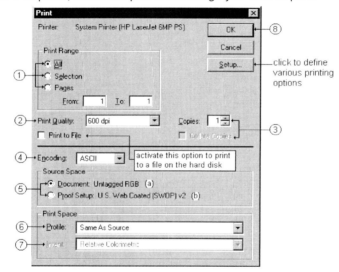

① If your image takes up several pages, specify which pages you wish to print. If a rectangular selection is present on the image, you can print just that area by ticking the **Selection** option.

② Give the print quality in dpi (dots per inch). The options given here depend on your printer.

③ If necessary, enter the number of copies you want to print. The **Collate Copies** option sorts the printed pages into separate copies.

④ If you are printing to a PostScript printer, define the **Encoding** to be used:

ASCII Select this option if you are printing from a PC or if you have printing problems.

Binary Use this option if you are printing from a Macintosh.

JPEG Avoid using this option as it reduces the print quality, even though you will print more quickly. Level 1 PostScript printers must not use this option.

⑤ Select the source colour space:

(a)   Uses the colour profile defined in the document to reproduce colours.

(b)   Uses the CMYK profile selected in the Photoshop colour profile.

⑥ Define the **Profile** option to print using your computer's colour space:

Same As Source: prints using the colour conversion defined by the document's colour profile.

PostScript Color Management: use this option if you are using a Level 2 or higher PostScript printer. For CMYK images, select this option if your printer is at least PostScript Level 3, otherwise choose the **Lab Color** option.

Printer Color Management: use this option if you are printing on a non-PostScript printer. If you have a specific profile for your printer's colour space, make this your preferred choice.

⑦ Depending on the profile being used, you can specify a rendering intent, used when converting colours between different spaces:

Perceptual: may modify the colour values but aims to give the most similar result as perceived by the human eye. This intent is useful for photographs.

Saturation: changes the hue, giving emphasis to the saturation of colours, which produces strong bright colours even though the hue accuracy is reduced. Use this intent when printing graphics.

Absolute Colorimetric: keeps precise colours without taking their perception into account. This produces a better result if the image's white point information (for very light tones) is accurate.

Relative Colorimetric: attempts to achieve a balance between colour accuracy and correct perception. **Perceptual** intent is often used for photos but this intent can also be used if you are seeking better colour accuracy. This is the intent used by default.

⑧ Click to start printing.

B-Defining page setup

File - Page Setup or `Ctrl` `⇧ Shift` **P** (PC) or `⌘ ⌦` `⇧ Shift` **P** (Mac)

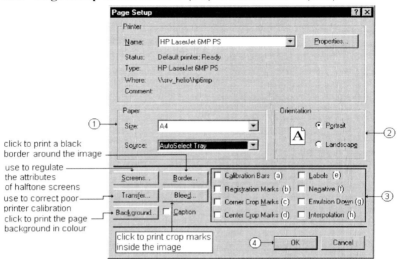

① Specify the paper size that you wish to use for printing.

② Select the appropriate page orientation for the item you are printing.

③ Using the various check boxes, specify the elements that are to be printed with the image:

(a)   prints CMYK and RGB colours plus a CMYK colour bar. This option requires a PostScript printer.

(b)   prints registration marks for aligning colour films. This option is only useful when printing with colour separation (primarily used by professional printers).

(c)   prints cropping guides on corners where the page will be trimmed.

(d)   identical to the previous option, but prints the crop marks in the centre.

(e)   prints the document name. If a single layer is active, its name will also be printed.

(f)   prints a negative of the image.

(g)   specifies when the light-sensitive side of a film is face down. This option requires a PostScript printer.

(h)   resamples a low-resolution image to reduce the jagged appearance that often occurs. This option requires a PostScript printer.

④ Click **OK**.

⇨ *To check whether the image will fit on the page, click (and hold the mouse button) at the place on the status bar where the document size is shown.*

C-Defining the print options

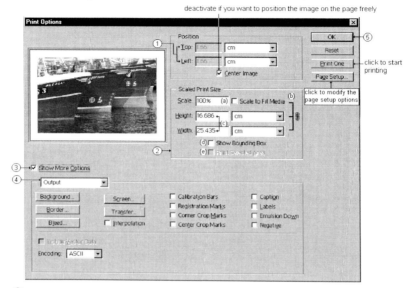

deactivate if you want to position the image on the page freely

① Define the top and left margins.

② Change the printing size by defining one of the following options:

(a) prints a larger or smaller scaled version of the image, according to this percentage.

(b) fits the image as best it can on the page; this also changes the **Scale** value.

(c) prints the image according to the width and height specified here.

(d) lets you define the printing scale manually. A frame with selection handles (the bounding box) appears in the preview box, drag a handle to reduce or increase the printing size.

(e) limits printing to an area you selected previously with the selection rectangle tool.

③ If required, tick this option to see and use the full list of options concerning page setup, output and colour management.

④ Select the type of options you wish to define:

Output to define setup options. If your image contains vector paths or text, tick the **Include Vector Data** option to use the maximum resolution from a PostScript printer on these items even if the image resolution is lower. Select the required type of **Encoding**: **ASCII** on a PC, **Binary** on a Mac, avoiding the **JPEG** encoding which reduces print quality.

Color to define the colour space you want to use for prin-
Management ting.

⑤ Click to confirm.

▷ *Scaling the printed size of a document, no matter which method you choose, does not alter the actual image size. If the image is imported into another application, it will keep its size.*

2.3 History

A-Managing the History palette

The History palette stores the last actions performed and allows you to cancel several successive commands or to retouch a previous state of the image.

Looking at the History palette

▓ **Window** Click the **History** tab
Show History

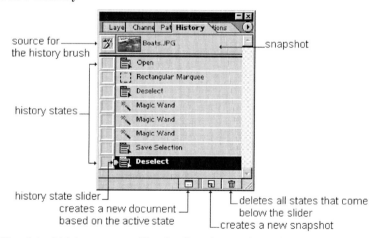

source for the history brush

snapshot

history states

history state slider

creates a new document based on the active state

deletes all states that come below the slider

creates a new snapshot

The list of history states, like the list of snapshots, is shown in chronological order.

▷ *The palette contents are not saved with the document and are only valid for your current work session.*

Undoing several actions

If the **History** palette is hidden, show it.

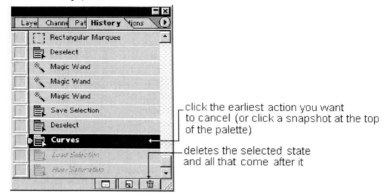

click the earliest action you want to cancel (or click a snapshot at the top of the palette)

deletes the selected state and all that come after it

The cancelled operations are still visible but are greyed-out. As long as you do not carry out any new work, you can still move the selection slider onto any cancelled actions to redo them.

⇨ *To cancel the deletion of states, use **Edit - Undo Delete States** or* Ctrl *Z (PC) or* ⌘ *Z (Mac).*

⇨ *To empty the history, use the **Clear History** command or* Ctrl *-click the* 🗑 *button on the palette: only states are erased, any snapshots are saved.*

⇨ *To remove items from the memory permanently, use the options in the **Edit - Purge** menu.*

⇨ *You can define the history preferences using the **History Options** in the palette menu.*

B-Creating snapshots of images

*The **History** palette allows you to create snapshots of an image, that is a saved version of the image at a particular stage of development or modification. Snapshots can be used to return to an intermediate stage of working on the image.*

Defining a simple snapshot

Show the **History** palette then click the ◧ button.

If you do not see the top part of the palette reserved for snapshots, increase the height of the palette.

new snapshot

- You can rename a snapshot by double-clicking its thumbnail: enter the new **Name** and click **OK**.

  The snapshot is renamed but all the states are cancelled, because they appear greyed-out. However, the image is not modified because the selection slider is positioned on the renamed snapshot.

- If the states that have just been cancelled may still be of some use to you, click the last state in the **History** palette or drag the slider to the bottom of the list.

⇨ *To delete a snapshot, simply drag it onto the* 🗑 *icon on the palette.*

Defining a specific snapshot

- Show the **History** palette.

- Activate the **New Snapshot** command in the palette menu (▶) or ![Alt]-click (PC) or ⌐-click (Mac) the 🔳 button on the palette.

- Enter the **Name** of the new snapshot.

- In the **From** list, choose between:

  Full Document   takes the snapshot with all layers stored separately.

  Merged Layers   takes a snapshot of the flattened image, that is, without taking into account the various layers which are seen as one single image.

  Current Layer   takes a snapshot of the active layer only.

- Click **OK** to save the new snapshot.

⇨ *To create a document from a state or snapshot, select the state or snapshot you want to use then click the* 🔳 *button in the **History** palette.*

C-Reproducing a previous state or snapshot

Using the history brush

▓ Show the **History** palette.

▓ Choose which state or snapshot will be the reference for your duplication by clicking it in the first column on the palette.

▓ Activate the  tool.

Lset the blending mode and tool opacity

① Click this button then select **Fade** in the **Size** and **Opacity** options to use the tool with a gradient that fades to zero width or to transparency.

② Open the palette of brushes and choose the required tool size.

▓ Drag over the areas of the image you wish to replace.

⇨ *If you click the ✎ icon in the first column of the **History** palette, you can no longer use the tool. To reactivate it, simply click the first column of a state or snapshot.*

Using the fill command

▓ Show the **History** palette.

▓ Click in the first column on the palette to define the source state or snapshot for the reproduction.

▓ If necessary, make a selection to limit the areas filled then use the **Edit - Fill** command or ⇧ Shift ⎯ .

▓ Select the **History** option in the **Use** box.

▓ Adjust the **Opacity** and blending **Mode**.

▓ Tick the **Preserve Transparency** option to fill only the visible pixels on the layer.

D-Reproducing a snapshot/state with an art effect

▓ Show the **History** palette.

▓ Choose which state or snapshot the reproduction will be based on, as with the  tool.

▓ Activate the tool.

① Set the painting mode and the opacity for the tool.

② Select a painting style to define the form of the line.

③ Set the colour fidelity.

④ Define the area covered by the tool (between 0 and 500).

⑤ Set the tolerance to limit the parts of the image affected by the tool.

⑥ Select **Fade** in the **Size** and **Opacity** options to use the tool with a gradient that fades to zero width or to transparency.

⑦ Select a tool size.

▓ Drag over the parts of the image to which you want to apply the stylised painting effect.

3.1 Channels

A-Using the Channels palette

Each image is made up of one or more channels; each channel contains colour information.

Window
Show Channels

Click the **Channels** tab

composite channel

click the eye icon
to show/hide
the channel

opens
the palette menu

loads a selection
saves a selection

deletes a channel
creates a new channel

- To activate a channel, click its thumbnail or name. All the selections, transformations or retouches as well as any moves made will be made on this channel and will not affect the others.

- You can also activate several channels by holding down ⇧Shift and clicking each of the channels that you want to modify simultaneously.

⇨ *An image can contain special channels such as alpha channels and spot channels.*

⇨ *Colour channels are by default displayed in the palette in grayscale. You can display them in colour by using the **Edit - Preferences - Display & Cursors** command and then activating the **Color Channels in Color** option.*

B-Using alpha channels

Creating a new alpha channel

- Click the ▣ button on the **Channels** palette. If you wish to define the new channel's options directly, Alt-click (PC) or ⌥-click (Mac) this button or select the **New Channel** command in the **Channels** palette menu (▶).

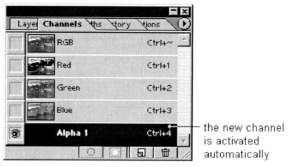

the new channel is activated automatically

▓ Make any necessary modifications to this channel.

▷ *You can have up to 24 channels in an image. The colour channels are included in this number.*

Creating an alpha channel from a selection

▓ Create a selection with the tool of your choice.

▓ Save the selection by clicking the ▣ button on the **Channels** palette.

To define the channel options directly, ⌐Alt⌐-click (PC) or ⌐⌐-click (Mac) this button.

A new channel corresponding to the selection appears in the palette.

Loading a selection from an alpha channel

▓ Activate the alpha channel containing the selection you wish to retrieve then click the ▣ button on the **Channels** palette or ⌐Ctrl⌐-click (PC) or ⌐⌐-click (Mac) the channel thumbnail.

▓ If required, show the image in colour again by clicking the composite channel thumbnail or by ⌐⌐Shift⌐-clicking the alpha channel thumbnail.

▷ *You can also use the **Select - Load Selection** command or drag the channel's thumbnail onto the ▣ button.*

▷ *To add the alpha channel selection to an existing selection, hold down ⌐Ctrl⌐⌐Shift⌐ (PC) or ⌐⌐ ⌐Shift⌐ (Mac) then click the alpha channel thumbnail.*

▷ *To subtract the alpha channel selection from the existing selection, hold down ⌐Ctrl⌐⌐Alt⌐ (PC) or ⌐⌐⌐⌐ (Mac) then click the alpha channel thumbnail.*

▷ *To load a selection corresponding to the intersection between the alpha channel and the existing selection, hold down ⌐Ctrl⌐⌐Alt⌐⌐Shift⌐ (PC) or ⌐⌐⌐⌐⌐Shift⌐ (Mac) then click the alpha channel thumbnail.*

LAYERS AND CHANNELS

C-Using spot channels

In addition to alpha channels, Photoshop allows you to create spot channels, used when printing with spot or special colours.

Creating a new spot channel

▨ If necessary, make a conversion to CMYK mode, grayscale or even multichannel mode.

▨ Show the **Channels** palette.

▨ If needed, make a selection so that the future spot channel only recognises the selected areas as areas containing the spot colour.

▨ Choose the **New Spot Channel** option in the **Channels** (🕥) palette menu or Ctrl-click (PC) or ⇧ ⌘-click (Mac) the 🔲 button on the palette.

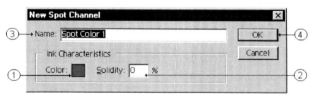

① Click the colour sample box to determine the spot colour you want to use. Click the **Custom** button to choose a predefined custom colour, such as one of the Pantone colours.

② Specify the colour solidity between 0 and 100%. This option merely allows a visual simulation of the spot colour on the screen and does not affect the printed result.

③ If required, choose a name for your spot channel.

④ Click to create the channel.

A new channel appears in the palette. Black areas on a spot channel are printed in the selected colour and the white areas are left empty.

⇨ *You can modify the spot colour by accessing the channel options as for an alpha channel.*

⇨ *If you need to use a selective varnish that will only cover part of the image, create a spot channel using any colour and name this channel* **Varnish**.

⇨ *You can use the drawing tools to retouch a spot channel exactly as you would for an alpha channel.*

Converting an alpha channel to a spot channel

░ In the **Channels** palette, activate the alpha channel you wish to convert.

░ Double-click the channel thumbnail or use the **Channel Options** command in the **Channels** palette menu (▶).

░ Activate the **Spot Color** option then set the **Color** and **Solidity** required for that spot colour channel.

░ Click **OK**.

⇨ *You cannot convert a spot channel to an alpha channel, unless you copy the contents of the spot channel and paste them onto an existing alpha channel.*

Merging a spot channel with the image

░ Activate the spot channel you want to merge with the colour channels of the image.

░ Select the **Merge Spot Channel** command in the **Channels** palette menu (▶).

░ If the image contains layers, you will have to flatten them. Click **OK** to merge the layers and the spot channel or click **Cancel** to stop the spot channel merge.

⇨ *You cannot merge a spot channel with a grayscale image.*

D-Modifying alpha channel options

░ Activate the channel that needs modifying then either select the **Channel Options** command in the **Channels** palette menu (▶) or double-click the channel thumbnail.

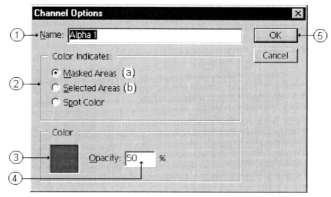

① Enter a name for the saved channel.

② Activate one of the following options:

    (a)   the selected areas are white on the alpha channel, the non-selected ones are black and partially selected areas are grey.

(b) the black areas on the alpha channel correspond to the selected areas and the white areas to non-selected parts.

③ Select a display colour for the channel by clicking the sample box.

④ Define what opacity the display colour will use for the black areas on the alpha channel.

⑤ Click to confirm.

E-Modifying a channel

▨ Activate the channel you wish to modify.

▨ Activate a drawing or retouching tool or use one of the retouch commands from the menus. You can also apply a filter to the channel to produce special effects.

▨ If you are using a tool, adjust its options.

▨ If you activated a drawing tool, select a drawing colour. If the channels are displayed in grayscale, use the following colours depending on the type of channel:

RGB color channels, Lightness channels in Lab mode, and alpha channels with **Masked Areas** option:

- **Black**: removes colour from the areas drawn on or filled. For alpha channels, the modified areas are removed from the selection.

- **White**: applies 100% of the drawing colour on the corrected areas. For alpha channels, the modified areas are added to the selection.

CMYK color channels, spot channels and alpha channels with **Selected Areas** option:

- **Black**: applies 100% of the drawing colour to the corrected areas. For alpha channels, the modified areas are added to the selection.

- **White**: removes colour from the areas drawn on or filled. For alpha channels, the modified areas are removed from the selection.

All colour, spot and alpha channels:

- **Grey**: applies a certain level of colour to the channel. For alpha channels, the filled areas will be partially included in the selection.

▨ Drag over the image if you are using a drawing or retouch tool. Define the settings if you are using a menu command.

▷ To delete the active channel, click the ⬚ button on the **Channels** palette or use the **Delete Channel** command on the **Channels** palette menu (⯈).

F- Duplicating a channel

You may want to duplicate a channel so as to make temporary copies and apply various effects.

▨ To duplicate the channel onto a new channel on the image, drag the thumbnail of the channel you wish to duplicate onto the [image] button on the **Channels** palette.

▨ To duplicate the channel onto an existing document, open this document (it should be as many pixels wide and high as the image currently containing the layer) then activate the channel you want to duplicate.

▨ Use the **Duplicate Channel** command in the **Channels** palette menu (▶).

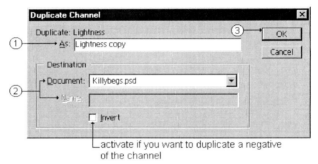

activate if you want to duplicate a negative of the channel

① Enter the new channel's name.

② Use this list to select the open document into which you want to copy the channel or a new document (in this case, enter a **Name** for this document).

③ Click to confirm.

⇨ *You can also duplicate a channel onto another document by dragging the channel thumbnail onto the window of the other document. This method also lets you duplicate a channel when two documents do not have the same number of pixels.*

G-Combining two channels

▨ Open, if necessary, another document to combine two channels from two different images.

This requires the two documents to be the same number of pixels wide and high.

▨ **Image - Calculations**

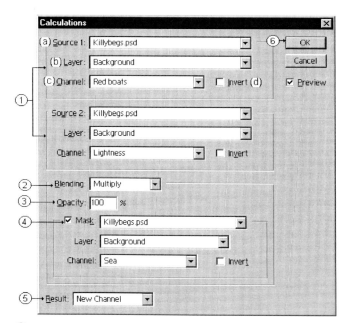

① For each of the channels you wish to mix, provide the following information:

   (a)   Indicate the name of the document that contains the channel to be mixed.

   (b)   Indicate on which layer the channel that you want to mix is located.

   (c)   Specify the channels that you wish to combine.

   (d)   Activate to combine the negative of the channel in question.

② Select the blending that you wish to use to combine the two channels. The **Add** and **Subtract** modes are specific to this command.

③ Set the opacity value. If it is less than 100%, the result of the blending will be softened and the **Source 2** channel will be dominant in the result.

④ If required, attribute a mask for the calculation. In this case you will have to supply the same information for this mask as for the **Source** channels.

⑤ Indicate how the result will be managed.

⑥ Click to confirm.

⤳ *Combining channels in this way does not allow you to combine composite channels. To do that, use the layers by adjusting the blending mode or use the **Image - Apply Image** command.*

H-Mixing colour channels

▧ If necessary, activate the layer on which you wish to make a correction or make a selection to limit the areas retouched.

▧ **Image - Adjust - Channel Mixer**

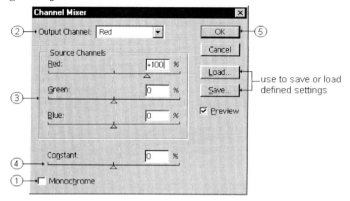

use to save or load defined settings

① Activate if necessary this option to prepare a high quality grayscale conversion or create specially tinted images.

② Select the output channel to which the channel mix will be applied.

③ Set the values on the source channels: a negative value inverts the source channel before mixing it with the output channel.

④ If required, modify this option to mix the output channel with an uniformly black or white channel: negative values equal a black channel while positive values equal a white channel.

⑤ Click to confirm.

I- Converting an image to multichannel mode

▧ If your image is an RGB or CMYK image in **16 bits/channel**, convert it to **8 bits/channel**.

▧ **Image - Mode - Multichannel**

▧ If your image contains layers, you will have to flatten the image.

The colour channels are converted into spot channels. In the case of a duotone, the two inks are separated onto different channels.

⇨ *On a colour image, the conversion to multichannel deletes the composite channel. The remaining channels vary depending on the colour mode.*

⇨ *If you wish to export a multichannel image to a desktop publishing application, for printing by a print shop, you should save the image in **Photoshop DCS 2.0** format. If you are using Pantone colours, you may have to save the names of the Pantone colours used in short form so they can be recognised. To do this, use the **Edit - Preferences - General** command and activate the **Short PANTONE names** option, then click **OK**.*

J- Merging channels into a single document

When you have a series of documents in grayscale, you can regroup them to make a colour image.

▓ If they are not open, open all the documents that you wish to merge. These documents must be in grayscale, have the same number of pixels across and down and possess no layers.

▓ Select the **Merge Channels** command in the **Channels** palette menu (▶).

▓ Select the type of image you want to create. If you modify the **Channels** option, putting in a value incompatible with the suggested **Mode**, the **Multichannel** mode will be chosen automatically.

▓ Click **OK**.

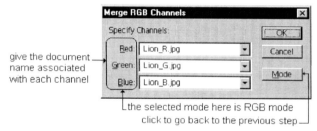

give the document name associated with each channel

└ the selected mode here is RGB mode
click to go back to the previous step ┘

▓ If you opt for a multichannel image, select the document name associated with the first channel then click the **Next** button to select the other channels. You will have to repeat this operation as many times as you want to add channels in the next step.

⇨ *If you select multichannel mode, all the channels are alpha channels and the resulting image is in grayscale.*

⇨ *You cannot separate then remerge an image containing spot channels. The spot channel will either be omitted during the merge or be placed as an alpha channel if you are merging on a multichannel image.*

⇨ *You can use this technique to merge an image digitised in grayscale through red, green and blue filters to produce a colour image.*

⇨ *Inversely, you can separate the channels of an image into distinct files using the **Split Channels** option in the **Channels** palette menu.*

3.2 Layers

A-Using the Layers palette

Photoshop documents (PSD name extensions) can be made up of several layers: this allows you to manage the different elements in the image independently.

▨ **Window**   Click the **Layers** tab
Show Layers

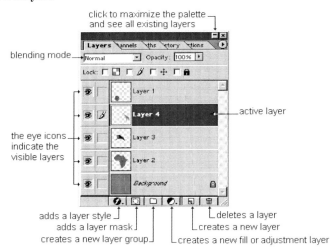

click to maximize the palette and see all existing layers

blending mode

the eye icons indicate the visible layers

active layer

adds a layer style
adds a layer mask
creates a new layer group

deletes a layer
creates a new layer
creates a new fill or adjustment layer

*The layer situated at the top of the list is the foremost layer on the screen, while the one at the bottom of the list is the one furthest in the background. The **Background** layer is the only one not to have transparent zones.*

▨ To activate a layer, click its thumbnail or its name.

B-Creating a new layer

▨ Activate the layer above which you want to insert the new layer.

▨ **Layer**   Alt-click the 🔲 button   Ctrl Û Shift **N** (PC)
New   ⌘ Û Shift **N** (Mac)
Layer   on the **Layers** palette

activate to add the layer to a clipping group

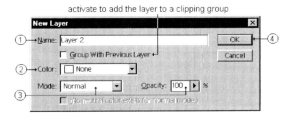

①→ Name: Layer 2   OK   ←④
☐ Group With Previous Layer
②→ Color: ☐ None
Mode: Normal   Opacity: 100 ▶ %
③→ ☐

① Enter the name of the new layer.

② If required, define the colour that will distinguish the layer in the **Layers** palette.

③ If required, define the other characteristics of the layer.

④ Click to create the layer.

⇨ *If the document does not have a background, you can create one using* **Layer - New - Layer from Background**. *The new background will be placed at the back, behind all existing layers and will be filled with the background colour.*

C-Changing a layer's properties

Select the layer concerned then use the **Layer - Layer Properties** command or hold down the ⌈Alt⌉ (PC) or ⌈⌐⌐⌉ (Mac) key and double-click the name of the layer concerned.

You can also open the **Layers** *palette menu (●) and choose the* **Layer Properties** *option.*

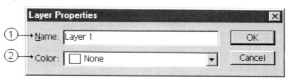

① Enter the layer name in the text box.

② If required, select a **Color** that will make the layer stand out on the palette.

D-Managing layers

To hide a layer, click the 👁 icon that corresponds to it. To hide all layers except one, hold down ⌈Alt⌉ and click the 👁 of the one that interests you. To display the layer again, click the small square to bring back the 👁 icon. To hide or show several layers, you can drag the pointer over the 👁 icon squares.

You can modify the size of the thumbnails in the palette by activating the **Palette Options** in the palette menu (click ●).

To change the stacking order of the layers, drag the layer concerned up the list to bring it closer to the front or down in the list to send it further to the back.

To duplicate a layer into the same document, point to that layer's thumbnail and drag it onto the 🔲 button on the **Layers** palette.

To duplicate a layer onto a different document, activate the layer you want to duplicate, then use the **Duplicate Layer** option in the **Layer** menu or on the **Layers** palette menu.

- To delete a layer, activate it then use the **Delete Layer** option in the **Layer** menu or in the **Layers** palette menu or drag the layer's thumbnail onto the [🗑] button on the **Layers** palette.
- To select a layer automatically with the Move tool, click the [▸₊] tool then on the options bar, activate the **Auto Select Layer** option. Now, when you want to move a layer, click a non-transparent area on the layer and it will be automatically activated.

⇨ *You can also use the options in the **Layer - Arrange** submenu to change the layer stacking order.*

⇨ *To duplicate a layer, you can also drag the layer towards the destination document.*

E-Managing layer sets

Creating a layer set

- Activate the layer above which you wish to insert the new set and click the [▢] button on the **Layers** palette.

  *A new set called **Set 1** appears in the **Layers** palette.*

- Activate the layer above which you wish to insert the new set and use the **Layer - New - Layer Set** command.
- Enter the **Name** for the new set and, if you wish, choose the **Color** that will make the set stand out in the palette.
- If required, define a blending **Mode** for the set. The **Pass Through** mode does not affect the blending modes applied to the layers in the set or the adjustments defined in adjustment layers. If you give a set a different blending **Mode**, all the layers within it will be affected and it could be applied in addition to the blending **Mode** already attributed to each layer. Adjustment layers will only work on elements belonging to that set. Lower level layers that do not belong to that set will no longer be affected by these adjustment layers. Advanced blending options will no longer produce the same effects. If you use these options, set **Pass Through** as the set blending mode so the effects do not stop at the set or **Normal** mode so the blending stops at the last layer within the set.
- If you wish, set an **Opacity** for the set. If you set the **Opacity** to a value less than 100%, all the layers within the set will be affected. The set's **Opacity** adds to that defined for each layer within the set.

⇨ *To integrate existing layers straight into a new set, first link these layers and use the **Layer - New - Layer Set From Linked** command.*

⇨ *To modify the properties of the active layer set, use **Layer - Layer Set Properties** (or double-click the name of the set) then make the required changes.*

Managing the contents of a layer set

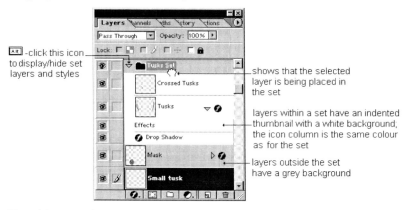

[ALT] -click this icon to display/hide set layers and styles

shows that the selected layer is being placed in the set

layers within a set have an indented thumbnail with a white background; the icon column is the same colour as for the set

layers outside the set have a grey background

▒ To add a new layer to a set, activate the set to which it should belong then create the new layer or adjustment layer.

▒ To transfer an existing layer into a set, drag the layer name onto the thumbnail of the set into which it should go. If you move the base layer for a clipping group in this way, the whole clipping group will be transferred to the layer set.

▒ To remove a layer from a layer set, drag its thumbnail out of that layer set's area.

▒ To change the stacking order of layers within a set, proceed as for an ordinary layer.

▒ To delete a layer set, proceed as for an ordinary layer. All the layers within the set will be deleted.

⇨ *You can also delete a layer or modify the stacking order of a layer within a set. To do this, proceed as if the layers were independent.*

F-Linking layers

▒ Activate, if necessary, one of the layers that need linking.

▒ Go to the other layer that you want to link and point to the small square situated to the right of the 🖌 icon.

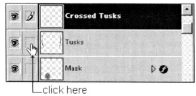

└click here

The 🔗 icon appears on the layer you chose to link; this is the symbol that the layer is linked with the active layer.

To delete a link, click the 🔗 icon again.

Be careful, simply activating another layer does not delete a link.

G-Aligning the contents of linked layers

Activate the layer which will be the point of reference for the alignment.

Layer - Align Linked or the options bar of the ⊞ tool.

Choose one of the first three alignments in the menu to align the layers along a horizontal axis or one of the last three to align them along a vertical axis. Alternatively, click one of the buttons on the options bar.

⇨ *You can use the* **Layer - Distribute Linked** *command to distribute the contents of several layers (at least three) to space them evenly.*

H-Merging layers

You can use this technique to group the items on several layers onto one single layer, thus reducing the size of the document.

Link the layers that you want to merge or mask the layers that are not to be grouped.

To merge two adjacent layers on the **Layers** palette, make sure there is no other layer linked with the active layer then use **Layer - Merge Down** or ⌃Ctrl **E**.

To merge all the layers linked with the active layer, use **Layer - Merge Linked** or ⌃Ctrl **E**.

To merge all the visible layers with the active layer, use **Layer - Merge Visible** or ⌃Ctrl ⇧Shift **E**.

Use **Layer - Flatten Image** to merge all the layers visible onto the **Background** layer.

I- Defining blending options for a layer

In the **Layers** palette, activate the layer whose blending options you want to adjust.

Layer   Double-click the layer
Layer Style   thumbnail
Blending Options

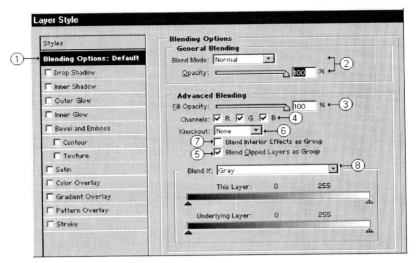

① Make sure that this option is selected.

② If required, set the **General Blending** options.

③ Set the background opacity to make the layer more or less transparent, like the **Opacity** option in the **General Blending** frame. The difference is that style effects applied to the layers will not be faded.

④ If required, activate or deactivate the available options. These vary depending on the image's colour mode.

⑤ Activate this option if you want the base layer of a clipping group to be the stopping point for blending when **Knockout** is applied to a higher layer. This option will have a similar effect on the last layer of a layer set. If you deactivate this option, the blend stops below the clipping group.

⑥ Define a knockout option for the layer. Many different factors affect how this complex option works: the blending **Mode**, the **Opacity**, the **Blend Interior Effects as Group** and **Blend Clipped Layers as Group** options for this layer and all lower layers all have a role to play in how it works. The presence of clipping groups and/or layer sets can provide stopping points for blending with the **Knockout** option. This option will give no result if you set the **Fill Opacity** to **100%**.

None: no **Knockout** occurs.

Shallow: **Knockout** occurs up to the first possible stopping point. This is determined by the last layer in a layer set or the base layer of a clipping group, in most cases. If no stopping point is located below this layer, **Shallow** knockout has the same effect as **Deep**.

Deep: **Knockout** occurs up to the image background or up to the next compulsory stopping point. This compulsory stopping point can be the last layer in a layer set or the base layer of a clipping group, providing the **Blend Clipped Layers as Group** option is active.

⑦ In a clipping group, tick this option if you want an effect applied to a layer in a clipping group to have a more limited effect on layers at the foreground of the group. If the **Blend Clipped Layers as Group** option is not active, the effect will only be applied to this layer.
This option does not work with the **Drop Shadow**, **Outer Glow** or **Contour** effects which work on pixels outside the layer.

⑧ In this area, you can make some areas of the layer transparent, depending on the brightness of the pixels present on **This Layer** or the **Underlying Layer**. Select **Gray** to work on transparency for all channels or pick a colour channel to work on transparency in that channel only. Drag the sliders to modify the layer's transparency:

Here is the image, before any transparency changes have been made. You can refer to this to see more clearly the changes made to the following examples.

This Layer: the black slider makes dark pixels on the layer transparent, if **Gray** is selected in the **Blend If** option. If a colour channel was selected, the dark pixels from that channel will be transparent:

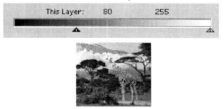

The white slider makes light pixels on the layer transparent, if **Gray** is selected in the **Blend If** option. If a colour channel was selected, the light pixels from that channel will be transparent:

Underlying Layer: the black slider will make dark pixels on the layers underneath show through, if **Gray** is selected in the **Blend If** option:

The white slider will make light pixels on the layers underneath show through, if **Gray** is selected in the **Blend If** option:

⇨ *The **This Layer** and **Underlying Layer** sliders are divided in two. To separate them, hold down* [Alt] *(PC) or* [⌐] *(Mac) before dragging them. This enables you to create softer transparency gradients on the areas concerned. To put the sliders back together, drag one of the halves to-wards the other half.*

⇨ *To associate a blending mode with a layer, select that layer then select the blending mode from the drop-down list at the top of the **Layers** pa-lette.*

J- Converting a background into a layer

▨ Double-click the **Background** layer thumbnail.

▨ Enter the layer **Name**.

▨ If you wish, choose the **Color** that will make the set stand out in the palette.

▨ Set the **Opacity** and the blending **Mode** for the layer.

*If this layer will be staying in the background without a new **Background** layer, you can use the **Opacity**, which will work normally. However, blen-ding modes will have no effect, except for **Dissolve** (if the layer has less than 100% **Opacity**), **Soft Light**, which will produce a grey result, **Color Dodge**, which will turn the layer black, and **Color Burn**, which will turn it white.*

K-Applying styles to a layer

Defining the global light for style effects

▨ **Layer - Layer Style - Global Light**

▨ Set the lighting angle between -180° and 180°.

▨ Set the **Altitude** for the lighting. This varies from 0 for a blinding light effect to 90 for light placed at the zenith.

You can also set these two values by dragging over this area in the dialog box.

▨ Click **OK**.

Applying and/or modifying a layer style

▨ Activate the layer to which you are applying the style. You cannot apply style effects to the **Background** layer.

▨ **Layer - Layer Style** or click the ▨ button on the **Layers** palette.

▨ Click the name of the style you wish to apply to the active layer.

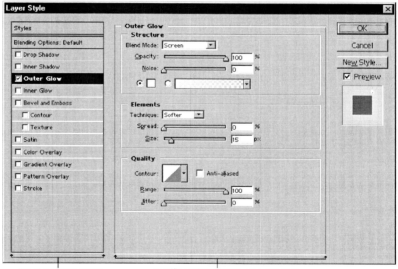

list of available styles   specific options for the selected style

▨ Tick the check boxes in the **Styles** column to apply those styles, or deactivate them to remove those styles.

▨ To show the setup options for a style to modify them, click the <u>name</u> of the style concerned.

Some examples of styles with various settings

The **Drop Shadow** effect applies a shadow to the outside of the layer and the **Inner Shadow** applies one just inside the layer with a variable **Distance** (generally between **10** and **30**):

Drop shadow
Distance=10

Drop shadow
Distance=30

Inner shadow
Distance=10

Inner shadow
Distance=30

The **Inner Glow** and **Outer Glow** effects apply a halo-like outline to the outside or inside of the layer depending on the **Technique** used (**Softer** or **Precise**):

Softer   Precise

The **Bevel and Emboss** effect with a different **Style** set in the **Structure** frame:

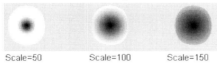

Outer
bevel

Inner
bevel

Emboss

Pillow
emboss

Stroke emboss
with added
Contour

The **Gradient Overlay** effect with a certain **Scale** of **Gradient** applied:

Scale=50   Scale=100   Scale=150

L- Managing style effects

As with layer sets, click the ⊳ icon to see the list of style effects applied or the ▽ icon to close the list:

click here to hide/display
all the layer effects

└ click here to hide/display the effect in question

To mask temporarily all the effects applied to all the layers, use the **Layer - Layer Style - Hide All Effects** command. Show them again with **Layer - Layer Style - Show All Effects**.

You can convert layer styles to layers using the **Layer - Layer Style - Create Layer** (or **Create Layers** as the case may be). You will no longer be able to modify the style's effects with the **Layer Style** effects in the **Layer** menu but you could retouch them using other methods.

M-Scaling style effects

When you apply layer style effects, their appearance often depends on the size of the object on the layer. If you resize the object, the effects applied are not modified. However, it is possible to scale the applied effects proportionally without affecting the object size.

Activate the layer whose style effects you wish to scale.

Layer
Layer Style
Scale Effects

Set the **Scale** to apply to the effects (this will generally be proportional to the scale applied to the object).

Click **OK**.

⇨ *This command is also useful if you copy effects from one layer to another or if you apply a style, as these may have been created for different sized layers.*

N-Managing layer styles

To apply a style, activate the target layer then go to the **Styles** palette and click the thumbnail of the style you want to apply.

To delete a style, drag that style's thumbnail onto the 🗑 button on the **Styles** palette or hold down Alt (PC) or ⌘ (Mac) and click the style's thumbnail.

To create a style, first apply or modify all the required effects to a layer or modify the advanced blending options then click the **New Style** option in the **Styles** palette menu (▶).

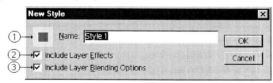

① Enter the new style's name into the appropriate text box.

② If required, deactivate this option to save only the blending options in the style.

③ If required, deactivate this option to save only the layer effects in the style.

⇨ *To rename an existing style, right-click (PC) or* ⌈Ctrl⌉-*click (Mac) the thumbnail of the style concerned then click the* **Rename Style** *option in the shortcut menu. Enter the style's new* **Name** *and click* **OK***.*

⇨ *You can* **Save Styles** *or* **Load Styles** *using these commands from the* **Styles** *palette menu (⊙). By default, these styles are saved in the \Program Files\Adobe\Photoshop 6.0\Presets\Styles folder.*

⇨ *You can also create a style by activating the layer containing the effects or blending options that you wish to incorporate into a style, then clicking the* ⌈🔲⌉ *button on the* **Styles** *palette. This method creates a style containing both the effects and the blending options from the selected layer.*

⇨ *The first style that appears in the palette removes all style effects and blending options from the active layer. It has the same effect as clicking the* ⌈🔍⌉ *button on the* **Styles** *palette.*

0-Creating a clipping group

A clipping group is used to make one image appear through the outline of a shape on an underlying layer.

▨ Show the **Layers** palette.

▨ If necessary, place the layer that will act as the mask under the layer(s) that are to be clipped. If several layers are to be in the group, they must be stacked one on top of the other.

▨ Activate the layer you want to clip on top of the masking layer. If several layers are to be clipped, you can link them to the masking layer so the clipping group can be created in one operation.

▨ **Layer - Group with Previous** or **Group Linked** or ⌈Ctrl⌉ **G** (PC) or ⌈⇧ ⌘⌉ **G** (Mac)

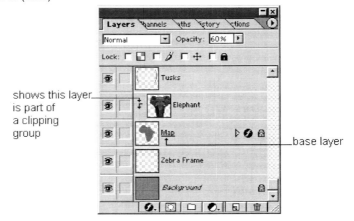

shows this layer is part of a clipping group

base layer

⇨ *You can add a layer to an existing clipping group in the same way you created the group.*

⇨ *You can also create a group directly in the Layers palette: point to the line that separates the two layers. Hold down* [Alt] *(PC) or* [⌐] *(Mac) (the pointer should take this form:* ⬅🖐*) and click: the two layers will be grouped.*

⇨ *To remove a layer from a clipping group, activate the layer that you wish to remove from the clipping group and use* **Layer - Ungroup** *or* [Ctrl][⇧ Shift] **G** *(PC) or* [⌘][⇧ Shift] **G** *(Mac). If the layer selected is not the layer in the group foreground, all the layers in the group placed above it will be removed too. Activating the base layer will undo the whole group.*

P-Creating and modifying a layer mask

A layer mask allows you to mask certain sections of a layer without modifying the contents.

▦ Activate the layer that will be masked.

▦ **Layer - Add Layer Mask** then click:

Reveal All to leave the whole layer visible by default.

Hide All to mask the whole layer. The layer mask will be black.

Reveal Selection to reveal only the items on the layer which are included in the selection. The layer mask will be white on the selected zone and black on the rest.

Hide Selection to hide the items on the layer that have been selected. The layer mask will be black in the selected part and white on the rest.

indicates that the layer
mask is selected ————

layer mask thumbnail —

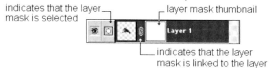

—— indicates that the layer
mask is linked to the layer

▦ Before modifying the layer mask, make sure that the 🔲 icon is displayed next to the 👁 icon. If you see the 🖌 icon in this place, it means that you are working on the layer itself.

To modify the layer mask, click its thumbnail to make the 🔲 icon appear.

▦ Change the layer mask using the drawing or retouching tools or by using certain filters.

- Apply black to completely mask the corresponding pixels on the layer.

- Apply grey to give a certain level of transparency to the pixels on the layer.

- Apply white not to affect the layer pixels at all.

▦ To make certain changes on the layer mask easier, you can show only the layer mask by [Alt]-clicking (PC) or [⌐]-clicking (Mac) its thumbnail. To show both again, perform the same task or click the layer thumbnail.

⇨ *You can also create a layer mask by dragging the layer thumbnail onto the* 🔲 *button on the Layers palette.*

LAYERS AND CHANNELS

⮒ *You can temporarily hide the effect produced by a layer mask by holding down* ⌊0 Shift⌋ *and clicking its thumbnail or using the command* **Layer - Disable Layer Mask***. The icon in the* **Layers** *palette will appear like this:*

⮒ *To redisplay the effect of the layer mask, click its thumbnail or use* **Layer - Enable Layer Mask***.*

Q-Applying or deleting a layer mask's effects

When you are satisfied with the effects produced using a layer mask, you can apply its effects to the layer then remove it.

▨ Activate the layer whose layer mask needs to be applied or deleted by clicking the layer mask thumbnail (the ▨ icon should be visible next to the ⊛ icon).

▨ Click the ⌊🗑⌋ button on the **Layers** palette

deletes the mask without applying its effects

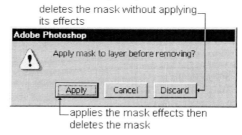

applies the mask effects then deletes the mask

⮒ *You cannot apply a layer mask to a Type layer. You must first convert it to a normal layer (meaning that the text can no longer be modified).*

⮒ *If you merge layers containing layer masks, the layer mask(s) are automatically applied then deleted.*

R-Creating an adjustment layer

An **adjustment layer** *can be used to make certain colour retouches to the image without modifying the pixels on the image. When you arrive at a satisfactory result, you can apply the layer to the image.*

▨ Activate the layer that will act as the reference for the adjustment layer. The adjustments made will apply to this layer and by default to all its underlying layers.

▨ If necessary, make a selection to limit the adjustment to one part of the image.

▨ **Layer**   ⌊Ctrl⌋-click the ⌊◖◗⌋ button
New Adjustment Layer   on the **Layers** palette

Select the type of adjustment required. You can choose from the same commands as can be found under **Image - Adjust**, except for automatic adjustments such as **Auto Levels, Desaturate** and **Equalize** as well as **Replace Color** and **Variations**.

If necessary, modify the layer **Name**.

Set the **Opacity** and blending **Mode** for the layer to tone down the effect.

Tick the **Group With Previous Layer** option if you wish to limit the adjustment to the previously selected layer. This creates a clipping group between the adjustment layer and the active layer. If the option is not ticked, all the layers underneath will be affected by the corrections made.

If you wish, define a **Color** that will make the adjustment layer stand out in the **Layers** palette.

Click **OK**.

The dialog box corresponding to the chosen adjustment appears.

Make the adjustment as required and click **OK**.

The adjustment layer appears in the palette, above the previously active layer. You should see an ⬚ icon, indicating that this is an adjustment layer. If the layer thumbnail is too small, another icon (⬚) will be displayed, no matter what the selected adjustment layer. If the ⬚ icon is present, it will change in appearance depending on the type of adjustment:

📊	Levels	🎨	Channel Mixer
📈	Curves	▓	Gradient Map
📊	Color Balance	◼	Invert
▓	Brightness/Contrast	▓	Threshold
📊	Hue/Saturation	▓	Posterize
📊	Selective Color		

When an adjustment layer is active, the ⬚ icon will appear next to the ⬤ icon, as for layer masks.

⇨ *If the adjustment is suitable, you can merge the adjustment layer with the layer underneath it. However in doing that you will make the adjustment permanent and you will not be able to modify it further.*

⇨ *If a selection was made before the adjustment layer was created, the layer thumbnail will show the selected area in white and the rest of the image in black.*

⇨ *To modify an adjustment layer, activate the layer concerned then use **Layer - Adjustment Options** or double-click the layer name. Make the necessary modifications. Click **OK**.*

⇨ *You can also modify the adjustment used by an adjustment layer by using the **Layer - Change Layer Content** command, then selecting the required adjustment.*

S-Creating a fill layer

As well as applying colour, gradient and pattern effects to modify an image, you can also use a fill layer to achieve a similar result.

▦ Activate the layer above which you wish to create the new fill layer.

▦ If required, make a selection to limit the fill to a specific part of the image.

▦ Click the button on the **Layers** palette.

▦ Select one of these options:

Solid Color   to apply a flat area of colour on the fill layer.

Gradient   to apply a gradient to the fill layer.

Pattern   to apply a pattern to the fill layer.

▦ Do the following, according to the chosen type of fill layer:

Solid Color: select the colour to be used for the fill.

Gradient: define the gradient options as if you were creating a standard gradient fill. In addition to these options, you can tick the **Dither** option to apply a gradient with softer transitions.

Pattern: define the pattern options as if you were creating a standard pattern fill. The **Link With Layer** option ensures that the pattern stays with the layer, if the layer is moved.

▦ Click **OK** to confirm.

*A special fill layer thumbnail now appears in the **Layers** palette.*

⇨ *You can also use the **Layer - New Fill Layer** command and choose the **Solid Color, Gradient** or **Pattern** option before entering a **Name** for the new layer. Next, tick the **Group With Previous Layer** option to create a clipping group (for which the layer you selected will be the base layer).*

⇨ *A fill layer is always associated with a layer mask. By default, this is defined by the selection you made before you created the fill layer. You can delete a layer mask on this type of layer but you cannot apply it to keep the visual effect it produces.*

⇨ *A fill layer cannot receive special adjustments, except for adjustment layers, nor can it be retouched by filters. You can apply all types of adjustment to the layer mask. If you wish to apply retouches to this type of layer, you will first have to convert it into an image using the **Layer - Rasterize - Fill Content** command.*
To modify a fill layer, proceed as for an adjustment layer.

T-Creating a layer clipping path

While layer masks create transparent areas on a layer, a layer clipping path performs similar actions, but from a vectoral path.

▓ Activate the layer on which you wish to create the layer clipping path.

▓ If required, activate an existing path to create a clipping path based on that path.

▓ **Layer - Add Layer Clipping Path**

▓ Select one of these options:

Reveal All: to create a new clipping path in which all the pixels on the layer will be visible by default.

Hide All: to create a new clipping path in which all the pixels on the layer will be transparent by default.

Current Path: to create a new clipping path in which the pixels covered by the selected path will be visible and the others will be transparent.

A thumbnail identical to the one used for a layer mask appears in the **Layers** *palette.*

⇨ *You can deactivate the effect of a clipping path temporarily using the* **Layer - Disable Layer Clipping Path** *command or by* ⬚ Shift *-clicking the clipping path thumbnail. To reactivate it, use* **Layer - Enable Layer Clipping Path** *or* ⬚ Shift *-click the clipping path thumbnail.*

U-Modifying a layer clipping path

▓ Activate the layer whose clipping path you wish to modify.

▓ If the drawn path cannot be seen on the image, show the **Paths** palette: a clipping path will be shown because the active layer contains a clipping path. Activate this path.

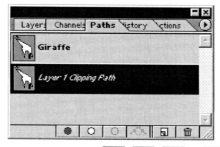

▓ Activate one of the following tools: ▚, ▚, ▚ or ▚.

▓ Modify the path as if it were a standard path (cf. 4.2 - H - Modifying a path).

The visible part of the layer is modified immediately according to your changes.

V-Applying or deleting a layer clipping path

▨ Activate the layer whose clipping path you wish to modify.

▨ Depending on the result you are seeking, activate one of the following commands:

Layer - Delete Layer Clipping Path: deletes the layer clipping path without applying the transparency effect it produces on the layer.

Layer - Rasterize - Shape: applies the effect of the layer clipping path to the layer; you can then retouch the outline areas. If this layer is a fill layer, this will also be rasterized. You cannot use this command if the layer clipping path is applied to an adjustment or type layer.

Layer - Rasterize - Layer Clipping Path: to transform the layer clipping path into a layer mask. This does not apply the effect, but simply transfers it to the mask. This may be useful should you wish to add a special effect to the mask before applying it. This is the only possible command you can use for layer clipping paths associated with an adjustment layer or a type layer.

The image is not modified but the layer clipping path thumbnail disappears from the Layers palette.

⇨ *You can also delete a layer clipping path by dragging its thumbnail onto the* 🗑 *button on the Layers palette.*

W-Locking or unlocking layers

▨ Activate the layer you wish to lock or unlock.

▨ Activate or deactivate one or more of the **Lock** options on the **Layers** palette:

⬚   to lock the transparent areas of the selected layer. All the non-transparent areas an be modified as you wish.

✐   to protect the layer from being retouched. All the drawing and retouch tools and filters become unavailable. However, transformations such as rotations and skews can still be made. This type of locking also causes the transparent zones to be locked.

✛   locks the layer's position. You can no longer move or transform it.

🔒   totally protects the layer. No further changes will be accepted. Apart from the three previous locks, you can no longer modify style effects, blending modes and opacity (cf. chapter 4). On a type layer, this type of lock prevents text editing.

⇨ *When a* ⬚, *✐ or ✛ lock is active on a layer, the* 🔲 *icon appears to the right of the layer name.*

⇨ *When the* 🔒 *lock is active on a layer, the* 🔒 *icon appears to the right of the layer name.*

4.1 Selections

A-Selecting a whole image

- **Select - All** or $\boxed{\text{Ctrl}}$ **A** (PC) or $\boxed{\text{⌘}}$ **A** (Mac)
- To invert a selection, use **Select - Invert** or $\boxed{\text{Ctrl}}\boxed{\text{⇧ Shift}}$ **I** (PC) or $\boxed{\text{⌘}}\boxed{\text{⇧ Shift}}$ **I** (Mac).

⇨ *If the selection border bothers you, you can hide it by deactivating the* **View - Show - Selection Edges** *command or by pressing* $\boxed{\text{Ctrl}}$ **H** *(PC) or* $\boxed{\text{⌘}}$ **H** *(Mac). To show the border again, repeat the command or press the keyboard shortcut again. Keep in mind that hiding the selection border does not actually cancel the selection, it simply hides it.*

- To deactivate the whole selection, use **Select - Deselect** or $\boxed{\text{Ctrl}}$ **D** or $\boxed{\text{⌘}}$ **D** (Mac).

B-Selecting a regular part of an image

- Select the $\boxed{\vdots}$ tool or the $\boxed{\bigcirc}$ tool (which is one of the tools hidden by $\boxed{\vdots}$).
- Make sure the $\boxed{\square}$ button is pressed in on the options bar.
- Use the **Feather** option on the options bar to create a muted transition zone between the selected object and the pixels around it. The higher this value, the more blurred the outline will be, integrating surrounding pixels with varying degrees of transparency.

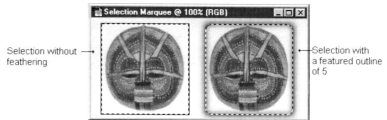

Selection without feathering →

← Selection with a featured outline of 5

- If the selection was made with the $\boxed{\bigcirc}$ tool, activate the **Anti-aliased** option to obtain a regular border without a staircase (or pixelation) effect on the selected item's border.
- Define the **Style** for the selection:

  Normal: to define the rectangular or elliptical selection with no constraints.

  Constrained Aspect Ratio: to define the rectangular or elliptical selection with width and height constraints. Select the ratio between width and height by entering values in the **Width** and **Height** text boxes.

SELECTIONS

Fixed Size: to define a rectangular or elliptical selection marquee of a specific size. Indicate the size in pixels in the **Width** and **Height** text boxes: the selection marquee will be drawn just by clicking the image.

░ Drag to draw a selection rectangle or ellipse. If you have chosen the **Fixed Size** option, just click the image.

░ Point inside the selection area and drag if the selection is not perfectly positioned.

The pointer takes this form:

⇨ *When creating a rectangular or elliptical marquee, you can make a perfectly proportioned circle or square by holding down* ⧉Shift *while you drag.*

⇨ *When creating a selection marquee, you can also use the* Alt *(PC) or* ⌐ *(Mac) key to draw the marquee (rectangle or ellipse) from the object's centre. Point to the centre of the object when you start dragging.*

⇨ *You can reposition the marquee while dragging by pressing* ⌷space⌷. *Release the* ⌷space⌷ *bar but not the mouse button to continue selecting.*

⇨ *For very specific tasks, you can use the* ⋯ *and* ⁞ *tools which allow you to select a single row or column of pixels.*

C-Selecting an irregular part of an image

Using the ⌐ tool

░ Activate the ⌐ tool.

░ Specify the **Feather** weight and tick or deactivate the **Anti-aliased** option, as for the ⌐ tool (cf. 4.1 - B - Selecting a regular part of an image).

░ Make sure the ⬜ button is pressed in on the options bar.

░ Activate the layer in which you want to make the selection then drag along the outline of the required section. To finish selecting, release the mouse button.

Using the ⋎ tool

░ Activate the ⋎ tool which may be hidden by the 🔍 tool.

░ Define the options as you would with the ⌐ tool.

░ Make sure the ⬜ button is pressed in on the options bar.

░ Activate the layer containing the item you are working on.

Proceed with a series of clicks to draw around the outline of the object. To finish off the selection, double-click or click the starting point (when you reach this point, the pointer takes this form:).

Using the tool

Activate the tool (which may be hidden by the tool).

Make sure the button is pressed-in on the options bar.

Use the **Width** option to specify the automatic detection area for the edges. This value can vary from 1 to 40.

You can modify the lasso width during the selection, by holding down the [or] key to increase or decrease the width by one pixel, respectively.

Use the **Frequency** option to specify the rate at which fastening points will be created. You can use a value between 0 and 100. For an image with low contrast, use a high value.

Use the **Edge Contrast** option to define the lasso's sensitivity towards the image's edges. If the edges are soft, use a higher value. If the edges change direction abruptly, enter a lower value.

Activate the layer on which the selection will be made.

Click to start outlining then drag the pointer over the object's edges. As you select, if you are unsatisfied with the selection, drag the pointer backwards. Press the Del key to remove the last fastening point. You can also click to create a fastening point manually. To finish off the selection, double-click or click the starting point (when this point is reached, the pointer takes this form:).

⇨ *You can deactivate the tool's magnetic properties temporarily. To do this, hold down Alt (or ⌥ on a Mac) and drag to make a selection portion as if using the tool, or proceed with clicks to select this portion as if using the tool. Release the key to retrieve the magnetic properties.*

⇨ *The **Stylus Pressure** option is only available if you have a graphics tablet. If you have one, activate this option to vary the width according to the pressure exerted. The higher the pressure, the narrower the width and vice versa.*

SELECTIONS

D-Selecting with Quick Mask mode

Defining the Quick Mask mode preferences

Double-click either the [icon] or the [icon] button on the toolbox.

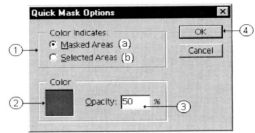

① Activate one of the following options:

(a)   if you draw in white on a mask, your selection is extended. If you use black, you remove pixels from your selection. Using grey, you make a partial selection.

(b)   this works in the opposite way to option (a). The areas drawn in white are removed from the selection and those drawn in black are added to the selection.

② Select a mask colour for the channel by clicking the sample box.

③ Define what opacity you want to use with the mask colour on the black areas of the mask.

④ Click to confirm your preferences.

Making a selection in Quick Mask mode

Check that the **Selection** mode is active on the toolbox: the [icon] button must appear pressed-in. If you wish, make an initial selection to limit the selection work in Quick Mask Mode.

Activate the Quick Mask mode by clicking the [icon] button on the toolbox (this button can also look like this: [icon]).

Activate a drawing tool to modify the selected area.

Adjust the tool options.

Select a drawing colour depending on the Quick Mask mode preferences.

Drag to paint the areas you wish to add to or take from the selection.

Once the selection is correctly made, click the [icon] button on the toolbox to return to **Selection** mode.

*The selection is active and the **Quick Mask** channel disappears.*

E-Feathering a selection

Select - Feather Selection or Ctrl Alt **D** (PC) or ⌘ ⌐ **D** (Mac)

set the feathering
width for the outline

F-Selecting an area of the image by colour

Activate the 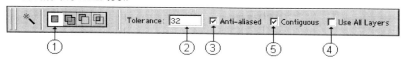 tool.

① Make sure this button is active.

② Specify the colour detection range (this varies from 0 to 255): the lower the tolerance rate, the more similar the colours have to be in order for the pixels to be selected.

③ Leave this option active to avoid a pixelation effect.

④ Activate this option to select zones that may not be on the active layer.

⑤ Leave this option active if you only want to select adjacent pixels. If this option is not active, all the pixels on the image taken into account by the **Tolerance** will be selected.

Click the required colour to select it.

⇨ *If there are "holes" of unselected areas, you can clean up the selection with the Select - Modify - Smooth command.*

G-Selecting a range of colours

Select the layer on which you wish to make the selection.

Select - Color Range

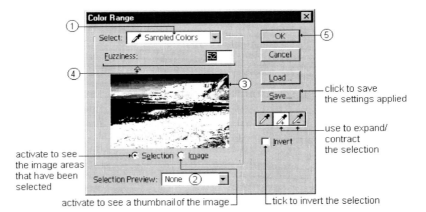

activate to see the image areas that have been selected

click to save the settings applied

use to expand/contract the selection

tick to invert the selection

activate to see a thumbnail of the image

① Use the **Sampled Colors** option to select an area on the image in relation to the colours of your choice, the **Reds/Yellows/Greens/Cyans/Blues/Magentas** option to select an area on the image in relation to a precise colour, the **Highlights/Midtones/Shadows** options to select in relation to the image luminosity or the **Out of Gamut** option to select all the colours that fall outside the CMYK colour spectrum. Only the **Sampled Color** option can be used on a selected area.

② Choose your desired type of selection preview.

③ Using the [tool icon] tool, click on a place in the image, or a place on the preview in the dialog box, corresponding to the colour you want to select.

④ Vary this value so as to take into account more or less similar colours.

⑤ Click to confirm.

H-Selecting non-transparent parts of a layer

Hold down `Ctrl` (`⌘` on a Mac) and, on the **Layers** palette, click the layer thumbnail whose selection you want to retrieve.

If a selection already exists, you can enlarge or reduce it by clicking a layer while holding down one of these:

`Ctrl` `⇧ Shift` (PC) `⌘` `⇧ Shift` (Mac)	to add the new selection to the existing one.
`Ctrl` `Alt` (PC) `⌘` `⌐` (Mac)	to remove from the existing selection the pixels corresponding to the new one.
`Ctrl` `⇧ Shift` `Alt` (PC) `⌘` `⇧ Shift` `⌐` (Mac)	to obtain a selection corresponding to the intersection between the existing selection and the new one.

Activate the layer whose selection you wish to retrieve.

Selection - Load Selection

In the **Channel** list, select **Layer Name Transparency**.

If the selection has previously existed, you can use a particular **Operation** option (cf. 4.1 - K - Loading a selection).

Click **OK**.

I- Expanding or contracting selections

Using the mouse

Hold down 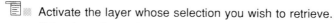 while using the selection tool to spread the selection out. You can also activate the ▣ button on the options bar. The pointer should have a small + sign attached.

Hold down Alt (PC) or ⌥ (Mac) while using the selection tool of your choice to reduce a selection. You can also activate the ▣ button on the options bar.

If you activated one of these buttons: ▣, ▣ or ▣ in the options bar, activate the ▣ button to return to simple selection mode.

⇨ *For more specific needs, you can limit the selection to the intersection between an existing selection and the current one. To do this, press Alt [⇧ Shift] (PC) or ⌥ [⇧ Shift] (Mac) while using a selection tool or activate the ▣ button on the options bar.*

Expanding a selection using its colours

Set the **Tolerance** for the ✎ tool on the options bar.

Open the **Select** menu and activate the **Grow** option to spread out the selection to neighbouring pixels, according to the tolerance used or the **Similar** option to spread the selection to all the pixels on the layer or the image which are similar in colour to those present in the selection.

Expanding/contracting a selection according to its border

To expand or contract a selection according to its selection border, use **Select - Modify - Expand** or **Contract**.

Set the expansion or contraction value for the selection.

J- Saving a selection

⬛ Selection - Save Selection

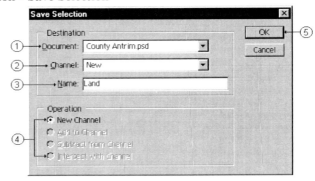

① Indicate in which document the selection should be saved.

② If a selection has already been saved, you can replace it with a new selection by choosing the corresponding option. To create a new channel, leave the **New** option active.

③ Give a title to the selection you want to save.

④ If you enter an existing selection in the **Channel** box, define how the two selections are to be combined.

⑤ Click to save the selection.

⤷ *This action creates an extra channel on the document, called an alpha channel.*

K-Loading a selection

⬛ Select - Load Selection

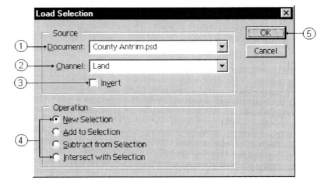

① Indicate which document Photoshop should look in to retrieve the selection.

② Choose the selection's name.

③ Activate this option to select all the image except the part which corresponds to the saved selection.

④ If the destination image already contains a selected item, specify how to combine it with the one you are about to load.

⑤ Click to load the selection.

⇨ *You can retrieve the last selection you have cancelled with the **Reselect** command in the **Select** menu, or by pressing* Ctrl ⇧ Shift *D*.

4.2 Paths

A-Creating a path

The Pen 🖊 *tool allows you to draw* **paths** *(or line drawings) that can be used to make precise and regular selections or to create a mask to clip an image. A path is not printed with the image (you can however apply a fill or stroke colour to a path).*

▨ Show the **Paths** palette.

▨ Click the 🔲 button on the **Paths** palette.

*A new path called **Path 1** is created in the palette. This path is automatically activated.*

⇨ *It is preferable to create a new path before drawing it. If you just begin drawing on the image, your path is considered to be a **Work Path**. This can be easily lost if you do not remember to save it.*

⇨ *You can also activate the **New Path** command on the palette menu (⊙) or* Alt *-click (PC) or* ⌥ *-click (Mac) the* 🔲 *button on the palette. This lets you name your path straight away by opening the **Path Name** dialog box for you.*

B-Creating custom shapes

▨ In the **Paths** palette, activate the saved path on which you want to work then use the **Edit - Define Custom Shape** command.

▨ Enter the **Name** for the shape in the corresponding text box then click **OK**.

*Photoshop creates a custom shape, which you can access from the **Shape** pop-up palette in the options bar for the* ✳ *tool.*

⇨ *You can rename or delete a custom shape, using the appropriate options from the palette menu (⊙) that appears on the **Shapes** pop-up palette.*

⇨ *You can **Save** or **Load** a custom shape, using the appropriate option from the palette menu (▶) that appears on the **Shapes** pop-up palette. By default, these shapes are saved in the \Program Files\Adobe\Photoshop 6.0\Presets\Custom Shapes folder. It is a good idea to keep saving them in this folder.*

C-Creating a path from a text

▨ Activate the type layer on which you wish to base the path.

▨ **Layer - Type**

▨ Depending on your required result, use one of these commands:

Create Work Path: to create a path whose shape corresponds to the text without affecting the type layer. This path is created as a work path; simply save it if you want to keep it. The text can still be modified normally.

Convert to Shape: converts the type layer to a fill layer associated with a layer clipping path, which takes the same shape as the text. The text can no longer be modified.

The type layer thumbnail is replaced by a fill layer thumbnail, associated with a layer clipping path.

D-Aligning or distributing paths

▨ In the **Paths** palette, activate the saved path on which you want to work.

▨ Activate the [⬉] tool.

▨ Click to select the path, or paths, that you wish to align or distribute. To select several paths, hold down [⇧ Shift] and click them. You cannot select paths situated on different saved paths.

▨ To align the selected paths, click one of the following tools on the options bar: ⬚̄ , ┨̄◻ , ⬚̄ₒ , ┃⬚ , ⬚̄ or ⬚̄| (cf. 3.2 - G - Aligning the contents of linked layers).

▨ To distribute the selected paths evenly, click one of the following tools on the options bar: ⊟ , ⊟ , ⊟ , ᑭᖯ , ᑫᑲ or ᑫᑫ. You must select at least three paths to be able to use this feature.

E-Using the freeform pen

Activate the  tool, which may be hidden by the tool.

(a)(b) ② ③
①

① Activate one of the following buttons:

(a)   to create a shape layer. This is a fill layer using the foreground
       colour and which is associated with a layer clipping path. The
       path will be visible in the **Paths** palette if the layer, once created,
       is selected in the **Layers** palette. If you activate this button, the
       options bar changes:

(b)   to create a vectorial path that will only be accessible via the
       Paths palette.

② Set this option to a value from 0.5 to 10. The higher the value, the
   simpler and smoother the path with less anchor points. A lower value
   will respect your freeform drawing more faithfully but will not correct
   any kinks or uneven stretches of path.

③ Check that this option is not ticked.

If you activate the button in the options bar, select the **Layer Style**,
the blending **Mode** and **Opacity** that will be applied to the fill layer.

Drag on the image to draw the path as if you were using the tool. If
you release the mouse button before returning to the path starting point,
you will create an open-ended path. If you return to the beginning, the

pointer takes this form: and you will create a closed path.

Leave the **Auto Add/Delete** option active on the options bar to add or
delete anchor points while you are drawing. If you point to:

a curve: the mouse pointer takes this form: +. If you click, a new anchor point is added to the curve, without modifying it.

an anchor point: the mouse pointer takes this form: –. If you click, the
anchor point is deleted from the path, which will modify it.

If necessary, continue the path by pointing to one of its ends. Depending

on the active pointer preferences, the pointer will appear as: / or ¯;¯.
Drag again from the chosen point.

*When you continue an existing path, you may find it does not represent
the path you dragged very accurately. This occurs because of smoothing,
but mostly because picking up the path creates a corner point.*

F- Using the magnetic pen tool

▨ Activate the 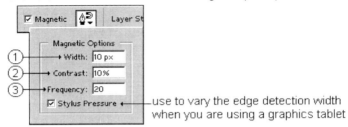 tool.

▨ Define the ⬚ tool options (cf. 4.2 - E - Using the freeform pen).

▨ Tick the **Magnetic** option.

▨ Click the ⬚ button to define the magnetic pen options.

use to vary the edge detection width
when you are using a graphics tablet

① Determine the automatic edge detection width, from 1 to 40. You can change the pen's **Width** while you are drawing by holding down the [or] key to increase or decrease the width by one pixel, respectively.

② Define how sensitive the "magnet" is to the image edges. If the outline is soft, use a high value.

③ Define how frequently the fastening points are created, from 5 to 40. This option works in the opposite way to that of the ⬚ tool.

▨ Click to start the path then drag along the path you wish to draw. While dragging, you can drag the pointer backwards if you are not satisfied with the last sections drawn. Press the Del key to delete the last fastening point. You can also click to create an extra fastening point.

▨ To complete your path, click back at the starting point. The mouse pointer takes this form: ⬚. You can also double-click to close the path with a magnetic segment or Alt (PC) or ⊏⊐ (Mac) double-click to close the path with a straight segment. Although this tool is not really adapted to creating open paths, you can create one by pressing Enter, which ends the path where the pointer is.

G- Using the pen tool

Setting options for the pen tool

▨ Activate the ⬚ tool.

▨ Depending on your desired result, activate the ⬚ tool to create a shape layer or the ⬚ tool to create a vectorial path.

▨ Click the place on the image where the path should start.

The path's first anchor point appears.

Select the option that shows how the path will react when several drawn paths overlap on the same saved path or when there is an intersection in the path:

 To create a larger shape. If the path is filled with a colour, the entire surface covered by the paths will be filled. If you export to EPS or DCS format, all the areas covered by the paths will be visible (cf. Clipping an image).

 to create a negative shape between the two paths. If the path is filled, the surface of the image except the area of the two paths will be filled.

 to create a shape from the intersection between the two paths. If the path is filled, only the intersection between the paths will be filled.

 to create a negative shape from the intersection (the opposite of the effect above). If the path is filled, all the areas covered by the paths except the intersections will be filled. This is the default mode used to create holes in shapes.

The thumbnail of each path differs according to the chosen method.

Leave the **Auto Add/Delete** option active on the options bar to add or delete anchor points while you draw.

Tick the **Rubber Band** option if you wish to see a preview of the next segment that will be created the next time you click or drag. This can help you draw a path more quickly.

Drawing straight lines

Click the place on the image where you want your path to begin then click the place where the other end of the line should appear. If you want to draw a perfectly horizontal or vertical line, or a line along a 45° angle, hold down ⓪ Shift before you click.

A straight line appears with an anchor point at each end.

Continue this path by clicking the place where the end of the next segment should fall. To close the path, click the first anchor point. The mouse pointer should take this form: ♟o. If you wish to make an open path, hold down Ctrl (PC) or ⓪ ✱ (Mac) and click anywhere on the image except on the path itself, or click the ♟ tool again.

Extending an existing path

If necessary, activate the path you wish to extend by clicking its thumbnail in the **Paths** palette then activate the ♟ tool.

Point to one of the path's ends (the mouse pointer should take one of these shapes: ♟□ or ⁻¦⁻, depending on the pointer preferences). Should the pointer have this form: ⁻¦⁻, make sure you point to the end very precisely or you may create another path.

■ Click to continue drawing with a straight segment or drag to continue with a curve.

If the path has been continued correctly, all the anchor points on the path should be displayed. If this is not the case, press Esc *then use the **Edit - Undo New Anchor Point** command.*

■ Continue your drawing by defining all the anchor points you think necessary.

■ Close the path by clicking or dragging on the first anchor point. The pointer should look like this: ⬝○. Leave the path open by holding down Ctrl (PC) or ⬝⬝ (Mac) and clicking elsewhere on the image or by clicking the ⬝ tool again.

Drawing curves

■ If necessary, activate the ⬝ tool.

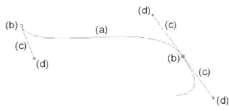

*A **segment (a)**, straight or curved, is defined by two **anchor points (b)**. In the case of a curve, **direction lines (c)** determine the curve's direction and slope. At each end of the direction line there is a **direction point (d)**. This is the point that you will work with to act upon the direction line when you want to modify the curve.*

To define a curve, proceed by clicking and dragging: the first click defines the anchor point position and as you drag, you move the direction lines arising from that point.

■ Click (and hold down the mouse button) the place on the image where your curve should start and drag the pointer in the direction that the path should take. Hold down ⬝ Shift as you drag to constrain the direction lines to move horizontally or vertically or at a 45° angle.

■ Click (holding down the mouse button) the place where the other extremity of the curve will be and drag the pointer so the curve is correctly defined. Depending on where you dragged the first anchor point and the direction in which you are now dragging, you will obtain very different curves.

dragging in the opposite direction

dragging in the same direction

If you are not satisfied with the result produced by an anchor point, you can press $\boxed{\text{Ctrl}}$ *Z (PC) or* $\boxed{\text{⌘ ⌘}}$ *Z (Mac) to delete the last point.*

You can also modify a point once the path is finished, as a path can be freely modified.

▦ If necessary, drag the anchor point that you have just defined to increase or decrease the length of the direction line defining the next curve.

▦ Continue the path by clicking where the new anchor point should be or dragging the pointer to define the curve. To change the curve's direction suddenly, hold down $\boxed{\text{Alt}}$ (PC) or $\boxed{\text{⌐}}$ (Mac) and drag the anchor point to modify the direction line. Continue making the path.

$\boxed{\text{Alt}}$ - dragging
the anchor point

The anchor points created along the path are called **smooth corners (a)**. *The direction lines that extend from them are always opposite to each other which gives a smooth curve (as the curve follows the same slope). When direction lines are "folded back", in other words, follow the same direction, the anchor points created are called* **corner points (b)**. *A corner point is always made from a smooth point that you convert along the path using* $\boxed{\text{Alt}}$ *(PC) or* $\boxed{\text{⌐}}$ *(Mac).*

If you $\boxed{\text{Alt}}$*-click (PC) or* $\boxed{\text{⌐}}$*-click (Mac) and not* $\boxed{\text{Alt}}$*-drag the anchor point you will change the curve into a straight line.*

▦ To close the path, drag to the first anchor point. The pointer should take this form: 🖊ₒ. Hold down $\boxed{\text{Alt}}$ if this point should be a corner point. For the last curve of a closed path, you should drag in the opposite direction for the direction line that needs redefining. This action only applies to the first/last point on the path. If you wish to make an open path, $\boxed{\text{Ctrl}}$-click (PC) or $\boxed{\text{⌘ ⌘}}$-click (Mac) elsewhere on the image or click the $\boxed{\text{🖊}}$ tool again.

⇨ *While you are drawing, if you are not satisfied with the anchor point you have just placed, press* $\boxed{\leftarrow}$ *to delete it and place a new point in the right position.*

SELECTIONS

H-Modifying a path

▧ Activate the path you wish to alter by clicking its thumbnail in the **Paths** palette.

Selecting anchor points and segments

▧ Activate the ⬚ tool (in the same group as the ⬚ tool).

▧ To select a segment, click the segment.

If a curved segment is selected, the direction lines controlling the curve are also shown.

▧ To select an anchor point, click it.

The square representing the point becomes solid: any direction lines also appear.

▧ To select several points, press ⬚ Shift⬚ and click each anchor point you wish to select. You can also drag diagonally to draw an invisible rectangle around all the points to be selected.

▧ To select all the anchor points, press ⬚Alt⬚ (PC) or ⬚⌐⬚ (Mac) and click the path (the pointer should take this form: ⬚ +).

⇨ *You can deselect selected points by ⬚ Shift⬚ -clicking the point concerned or by clicking outside the path to deselect all the anchor points.*

Moving a segment or an anchor point

▧ Activate the ⬚ tool.

▧ To move a straight segment plus the anchor points defining it, point to the segment and drag it.

▧ To change the roundness of a curve, point to the curve and drag.

The anchor points do not move when you modify a curve, only the direction lines are altered.

▧ To move an anchor point, select it and drag it.

⇨ *You can also move a curved segment, without changing its magnitude, by selecting the two anchor points that define the curve and dragging one of them.*

Adding or deleting anchor points

▧ To add an anchor point, activate the ⬚ tool then click to add a point without changing the existing curve or drag to modify the direction lines associated with this new point.

▧ To delete an anchor point, activate the ⬚ tool then click to delete the unwanted point or drag to delete the point and correct the way the path is restructured.

Modifying a curve

- Activate the tool then click the curved segment you wish to modify or one of the anchor points to display the curve's direction lines.
- Drag one of the direction points. To modify the curve's magnitude, move the direction point to bring it closer to or push it away from the anchor point, trying not to modify the way the associated direction line is pointing. To change the slope of the curve, move the direction point while changing the orientation of the direction line.

Converting a smooth point to a corner point and vice versa

- Activate the tool then click the anchor point you wish to convert to display the direction lines that are attached to it.
- Activate the tool.
- To convert a smooth point into a corner point, drag one of the direction points to "fold" the direction lines associated with the anchor point.
- To convert a corner point into a smooth point, drag from the anchor point to place the direction lines opposite to each other again.

  This conversion also works on points that have no direction lines. This allows you to create these lines.

- To delete the direction lines from an anchor point, click the anchor point once. If the next anchor point has no direction lines either, a straight segment will be created.
- ⇨ *To open a closed path, select the anchor point where you want to open the path then press either* Del *or* ←.

I- Converting a selection border into a path

- To convert the active selection, attributing the default tolerance value, click the button on the **Paths** palette.
- To convert the selection and give a tolerance value, activate the **Make Work Path** command on the palette menu (⏵) or Alt-click (PC) or ⌘-click (Mac) the button on the **Paths** palette.

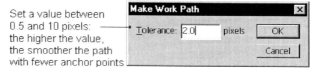

Set a value between 0.5 and 10 pixels: the higher the value, the smoother the path with fewer anchor points

J- Converting a path into a selection border

One of the uses of a path is to create a selection border rapidly. This action only applies to a closed path.

To convert a path using the default options, click the ⬚ button on the **Paths** palette or Ctrl-click (PC) or ⬚⌘-click (Mac) the path thumbnail.

To define the conversion options, activate the path you wish to convert by clicking its thumbnail then use the **Make Selection** command in the **Paths** palette menu (▶) or Alt-click (PC) or ⌘-click (Mac) the ⬚ button.

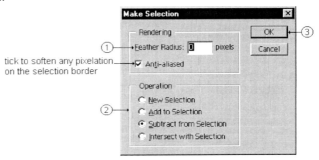

tick to soften any pixelation on the selection border

① Determine a feather radius between 0 and 250 (for a sharper or more blurred border).

② If a selection already exists on the image, indicate how to combine the existing selection and the one you are creating.

③ Click to make the conversion.

➪ *When a path is active, you can also define a New Selection with a Feather Radius of 0 by pressing the* Enter *key on the numeric keyboard while any drawing tool is active.*

K-Saving a work path

Show the **Paths** palette.

Double-click the **Work Path** thumbnail or activate the **Save Path** option in the palette menu (▶).

Enter the path's name then click **OK**.

L- Managing paths

Show the **Paths** palette.

To delete a path, drag that path's thumbnail onto the 🗑 button on the **Paths** palette or use the **Delete Path** command on the **Paths** palette menu (▶).

- To rename a path, double-click its thumbnail, enter the new name and click **OK**.
- To duplicate a path onto a new path, drag the thumbnail of the path you want to duplicate onto the 🔲 button on the **Paths** palette.
- To duplicate a path onto another image, drag the thumbnail of the path you want to duplicate onto the window of the document where you wish to place the copy.
- To hide or show all existing paths, deactivate or activate:

  View ⌈Ctrl⌉⌈⇧ Shift⌉ **H** (PC)
  Show ⌈⌘ ⌘⌉ ⌈⇧ Shift⌉ **H** (Mac)
  Target Path
- To deactivate a path, ⌈⇧ Shift⌉-click the active path's thumbnail.
- ⇨ *To delete a path, you can also activate the path you want to delete, then click the* 🗑 *button; you will then be asked to confirm your request.*

M-Transforming or combining paths

- In the **Paths** palette, activate the saved path on which you want to work.
- Activate the 🔺 tool.

- Tick the **Show Bounding Box** option so you can transform a path in the same way as a layer or selection.
- Click to select the path or paths that you wish to transform or combine. To select several paths, use ⌈⇧ Shift⌉-clicks. You cannot select paths located on different saved paths.
- If you want to apply a transformation, drag one of the selection handles. You can apply all sorts of transformations: rescale, rotate, skew, distort or perspective. To make a perspective effect, hold down ⌈Ctrl⌉⌈Alt⌉⌈⇧ Shift⌉ (PC) or ⌈⌘ ⌘⌉⌈⌐⌐⌉⌈⇧ Shift⌉ (Mac).
- To combine paths, select the required method in the options bar by clicking one of these tools: 🔲, 🔲, 🔲 or 🔲 (cf. 4.2 - G - Using the pen tool).
- Click the **Combine** button on the options bar to merge the combined paths. If you selected the 🔲 or 🔲 combining method, the intersections between the selected paths disappear to create a single path.

SELECTIONS

N-Applying colour to a path outline

⬜ Activate the layer on which you want to apply the colour or retouch.

⬜ Activate the path required for the fill or retouch.

⬜ Select the drawing or retouch tool that you want to apply along the path. You can use one of these tools: ⬛, ⬛, ⬛, ⬛, ⬛, ⬛, ⬛, ⬛, ⬛, ⬛, ⬛, ⬛, ⬛, ⬛ or ⬛. If you want to select the ⬛ tool, make sure you first define a duplication origin, otherwise Photoshop will show an error message and no effect will be made. If you activate another tool apart from those shown, Photoshop will use the ⬛ tool by default.

⬜ If required, modify the settings for the chosen tool in the options bar.

⬜ If you select a drawing tool, chose a foreground colour.

⬜ Click the ⬛ button in the **Paths** palette.

O-Applying fill colour inside a path area

⬜ Activate the layer or which you want to apply the fill colour, then the path that you wish to fill.

⬜ To apply colour using the default options, select a foreground colour for the fill then click the ⬛ button on the **Paths** palette.

⬜ To apply colour and define the options, select a foreground colour for the fill then ⬛-click (PC) or ⬛-click (Mac) the ⬛ button or activate one of these commands from the **Path** palette menu (⬛):

Fill Path: to apply a background colour to a path of which no anchor point or segment is selected.

Fill Subpath: to apply fill to a path of which at least one anchor point is selected.

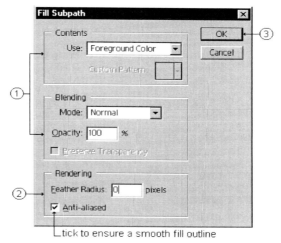

└ tick to ensure a smooth fill outline

① Define how the path should be filled.

② Specify a width for the feather radius of between 0 and 250 to control the sharpness of the fill's edges.

③ Apply the colour to the path area.

⇨ *If you fill an open path, the various meanders of the path will be filled in and the path will be closed off by a straight segment joining its two ends.*

5.1 Bitmap drawings

A-Selecting a colour

Using the Color palette

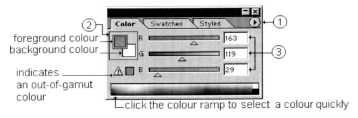

foreground colour
background colour

indicates
an out-of-gamut
colour

└click the colour ramp to select a colour quickly

① If the colour model does not suit your needs, open the palette menu (⏺) and choose the option you prefer.

② To choose a foreground colour, make sure that the colour selection box has a double frame around it (and is thus active). If this is not the case, click it once.

③ Drag the different sliders (△) to define each colour component or enter a colour value in the corresponding text box.

▷ *Click the box of the selected colour to open the Color Picker.*

▷ *To use another model, open the palette menu (⏺), activate RGB Spectrum, CMYK Spectrum, Grayscale Ramp or Current Colors (this option gives a gradient between the foreground and background colours). The Make Ramp Web Safe option restricts the colours shown in the colour ramp to those recognised by Web browsers in 256 colours.*

Using the Color Picker

▦ Click the foreground or background colour selection box on the toolbox or on the **Color** palette to open the **Color Picker**.

▦ If the dialog box shown is **Custom Colors**, click the **Picker** box to return to the **Color Picker**.

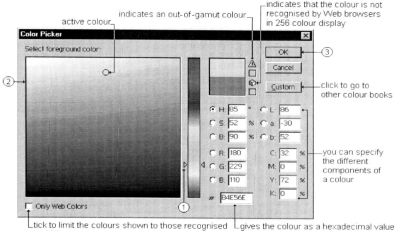

indicates that the colour is not recognised by Web browsers in 256 colour display

indicates an out-of-gamut colour

active colour

click to go to other colour books

you can specify the different components of a colour

tick to limit the colours shown to those recognised by 256 colour Web browsers

gives the colour as a hexadecimal value

① Drag the slider to select the hue.

② Click the colour field to select the desired colour.

③ Click to confirm.

Using the Swatches palette

▓ Show the **Swatches** palette.

▓ Click one of the colours to select the foreground colour. Hold down ⟦Alt⟧ (PC) or ⟦⌐⟧ (Mac) and click a colour to select the background co-lour.

Using the Eyedropper tool 🖊️

▓ Click the 🖊️ tool.

▓ On the options bar, select the size of the sample used for the eyedropper:

Point Sample: picks up the colour of the pixel that you click.

3x3 Average: takes a colour based on the average of the nine pixels surrounding the one you click.

5x5 Average: takes a colour based on the average of the twenty-five pixels surrounding the one you click.

▓ Click the part of the image whose colour you want to pick up to select the foreground colour. Hold down ⟦Alt⟧ (PC) or ⟦⌐⟧ (Mac) and click to choose a background colour. Be careful, the choice of foreground/background colours may be inverted if the **Color** palette is shown and if the back-ground colour selection box has been activated.

⇨ *The* **Info** *palette will show you the different colour components of the image as you move the pointer over it.*

IMAGE MODIFICATION

Using a custom color picker

▓ Open the **Color Picker** then if necessary, click the **Custom** button.

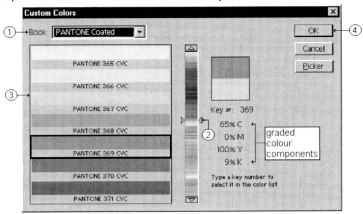

① Select a color system in the list.

② Drag the vertical slider to select a colour.

③ Click a specific shade or type in the colour reference.

④ Click to confirm your choice.

B-Drawing with the pencil, paintbrush or airbrush

▓ If necessary, activate the layer on which you want to draw or select a part of the image to delineate the drawing area.

▓ Activate one of these tools: Pencil ![pencil], Paintbrush ![paintbrush] or Airbrush ![airbrush].

▓ If necessary, select a blending **Mode**.

The various blending modes allow you to apply different effects.

▓ If required, change the stroke's **Opacity**.

*The **Opacity** option will be replaced by the **Pressure** option if you use the ![airbrush] tool. This controls how fast the paint accumulates.*

▓ Click the ![button] button on the options bar and select the **Fade** option under **Size** and/or **Opacity** and/or **Color** if you want to draw with a gradient that goes towards a zero width and/or to transparency and/or to the background colour. You can then specify the number of **steps** you want to use.

As with the ![pencil] tool, the number of steps for a fade varies from 1 to 9999. A value of 0 stops the fade.

*Tick the **Wet Edges** option (specific to the  tool) if you want to create a watercolour effect that spreads pigment around the brush outline:*

without
wet edges

with
wet edges

*When you use the ⟨tool⟩ tool, the **Auto Erase** option replaces the **Wet Edges** option. This option enables you to paint in the foreground colour if the pixels on which you start to draw are different than the foreground colour. If these pixels are already in the foreground colour, you will paint with the background colour.*

Select a foreground colour for your drawing. If you are using a fade to background, select a background colour too.

Select a brush type in the pop-up palette of brushes on the options bar.

Point to the place where you wish to start drawing and drag the pointer to draw. You can hold down ⟨û Shift⟩ as you drag to make a horizontal or vertical line. To draw lines along different angles (creating zigzags, polygons), hold down ⟨û Shift⟩ and draw by making a series of clicks.

C-Creating geometrical and preset shapes

Activate one of the following tools: ⬜, ⬜, ⚪, ⬡, ◥ or ✳.

tool-specific Geometry options

The options bar changes. If a drawing is active, only the options concerning shape combinations and the tool type are available. If no drawing is active, the combination types disappear from the bar but additional information appears, which you can modify.

Depending on your desired result, click one of the following buttons:

 to create a shape layer, which is a fill layer using the foreground colour and associated with a layer clipping path.

 to create a vectorial path that will be accessible only in the **Paths** palette.

 to create a shape filled with the foreground colour on the active layer but without creating any paths.

IMAGE MODIFICATION

Setting options for the Rectangle, Rounded Rectangle and Ellipse tools

▨ Click the ▭ or ▭ or ○ tool button then open the pop-up palette of **Geometry options**:

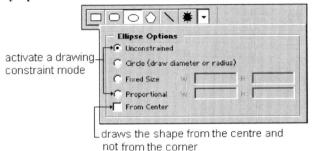

activate a drawing constraint mode

└ draws the shape from the centre and not from the corner

▨ If you select the ▭ or ▭ tools, tick the **Snap to Pixels** option if you wish the shape to start at the intersection between pixels.

▨ Set the **Radius** for the ▭ tool. This defines how rounded the corners will be. The **Radius** can vary from 0 to 1000 pixels.

Setting options for the Polygon tool

▨ Click the ⬠ tool button then open the pop-up palette of **Geometry options**.

▨ Define the **Radius** to create a fixed-size polygon. The polygon created like this will be twice as large as the value indicated.

▨ Tick the **Smooth Corners** option to round the polygon's corners.

▨ Tick the **Indent Sides By** option and enter a percentage value in the text box if you want to create a star shape.

▨ Tick the **Smooth Indents** option to curve the star's branches. This option is unavailable if you are not using the **Indent Sides By** option.

▨ In the options bar, give the required number of **Sides** for the polygon (between 3 and 100).

⇨ *Unlike the* ▭ *tool, you can turn the shape while you draw it. This means you could use this tool to create rectangles or squares with a certain rotation angle. To do this, make sure you specify four* **Sides** *for the shape.*

D-Setting options for the Line tool

▨ Click the 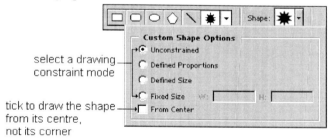 tool button then open the pop-up palette of **Geometry options**.

▨ Tick the **Start** and/or **End** options to create a line with an arrowhead at the start and/or end of it.

▨ If you create an arrowhead line, set these options:

Width: to determine what percentage (from 10 to 1000) the width of the arrowhead point will be in relation to the line.

Length: to determine what percentage (from 10 to 1000) the length of the arrowhead point will be in relation to the width of the line.

Concavity: to create a concave or convex curve on the widest part of the arrowhead. This value can vary from -50 to +50%.

▨ In the options bar, set the line **Weight** from 1 to 1000 pixels.

E-Setting options for the Custom Shape tool

▨ Click the ✳ button on the options bar then open the pop-up palette of **Geometry options**.

select a drawing constraint mode

tick to draw the shape from its centre, not its corner

Custom Shape Options
◉ Unconstrained
○ Defined Proportions
○ Defined Size
○ Fixed Size   W: H:
☐ From Center

▨ Select the **Custom Shape** you want to draw, by opening the pop-up **Shape** palette on the options bar and clicking the shape.

Setting the common options

▨ Select the **Layer Style** to apply to the custom shape layer. This option is only available if you choose to create the shape layer by clicking the ▣ button on the options bar.

▨ Set the blending **Mode** and the **Opacity** to apply to the layer. These options are only available if you choose to create the shape by clicking the ▥ button on the options bar.

▨ Tick the **Anti-aliased** option to draw shapes without any pixelation effect on the outlines. This option is available if you choose to create the shape by clicking the ☐ button on the options bar.

IMAGE MODIFICATION

Drawing a geometrical or custom shape

▨ Select the foreground colour, if you are creating the shape on a shape layer or on an ordinary layer (using the ⬛ or ⬛ tool on the options bar).

▨ Drag to draw your shape. With the ⬡ and ✎ tools, you can hold down ⬙ Shift to constrain to a 0°, 45° or 90° angle. For other tools, hold down ⬙ Shift to draw a perfectly proportioned shape such as a square or circle or a polygon with sides of the same length.

F-Deleting part of an image

▨ If necessary, activate the layer in which you want to delete something then activate the ✎ tool.

① Select an eraser tool to rub out the image.

② Use this option to rub out more or less superficially, in order to keep a certain amount of the rubbed-out pixels visible: if you select the **Air-brush** eraser tool, the **Opacity** option is replaced by **Pressure**. This acts similarly to **Opacity** but also produces an accumulation effect: the longer you stay in the same spot, the more the eraser will rub out.

③ Click this button and select the **Fade** option for the **Size** and/or **Opacity** options to erase as a gradient up to a zero **Size** and/or to zero opacity. The indicated value sets the distance after which the eraser will have no effect. This can vary from 1 to 999. To remove the fade effect, click the ✎ button and choose **Off** on the option concerned.

④ If you have chosen the paintbrush eraser, activate this option to give a watercolour effect when using the brush.

⑤ Activate this option in order to rub out in relation to the previous states of the image.

▨ If you have chosen any other eraser than the **Block** type, open the **pop-up brushes** palette then select an eraser brush type.

▨ Point to the item you want to erase and drag to rub out.

⇨ *There are also two other special eraser types you can use:* ✎, *the* ***background eraser*** *allows you to rub out part of an image and make it transparent. This works like an amalgam of the* ✎ *and* ✎ *tools. The* ***magic eraser*** ✎ *selects similar pixels with the same technique as the* ✎ *tool, then erases them to transparency.*

⇨ *You can also delete by making a selection then using* ***Edit - Clear*** *or* ⬚Del.

G-Describing blending modes

Blending modes determine how a drawing tool behaves when used. For layers, they determine how the elements on the active layer will be applied in relation to elements on underlying layers. You will also see that these modes can be used when applying filters, when adjusting images or for channels.

The result produced by these modes depends on two factors:

– The **base colour** corresponds to the image's original colour.

– The **blend colour** refers to the foreground colour, in the case of drawing tools. For layers, each pixel on the layer is considered as a specific blend colour.

*The blending mode applied with a **blend colour** over a **base colour** gives a **result colour**.*

Normal: the blend colour totally covers the base colour if opacity equals 100% (this mode is called **Threshold** when you work on Bitmap or Indexed Color images).

Dissolve: replaces the base colour by the blend colour in a random manner.

Behind: is identical to **Normal** mode for the transparent areas of a layer. On opaque areas, this mode has no effect and the base colour remains unaltered. On partially transparent areas, the blend colour is applied with a reduced opacity, proportional to the transparency of the base colour.

Clear: can only be used with the ⬚ and ⬚ tools as well as with the **Edit - Fill** or **Edit - Stroke** commands. It makes the layer areas you are working on transparent.

Multiply: as its name implies, this multiples the blend colour by the base colour to obtain the result colour.

Screen: this mode multiplies the negative of the base colour with the negative of the blend colour to achieve its result colour.

Overlay: this mode applies **Multiply** or **Screen** mode depending on the base colour. If that colour is lighter than the blend colour, **Multiply** mode will be used. If the base colour is darker than the blend colour, **Screen** mode will be applied. This mode preserves the base colour's luminosity.

Soft Light: this mode lightens or darkens the base colour, depending on the blend colour. If the blend colour has greater than 50% luminosity, the base colour will be lightened, taking into account the blend colour. If the luminosity is less than 50%, the base colour will be darkened.

Hard Light: this mode lightens or darkens the base colour depending on the blend colour. If the blend colour has more than 50% luminosity, a process similar to that in **Screen** mode will lighten the base colour. If the luminosity is less than 50%, a darkening will occur, much in the same way as with the **Multiply** mode.

Color Dodge: this mode lightens the base colour, taking into account the blend colour.

IMAGE MODIFICATION

Color Burn: this mode darkens the base colour, relative to the blend colour. This darkening occurs for each colour channel.

Darken: this mode uses the blend colour to darken the base colour; the two colours are not mixed. For each colour channel, the darkest colour is preserved.

Lighten: this lightens the base colour using the blend colour; the colours are not mixed. For each colour channel, the lightest colour is kept.

Difference: for each colour channel, this mode performs a subtraction between the base and blend colours. If the blend colour has a higher brightness value than the base colour, the base colour will be subtracted from the blend colour and vice versa.

Exclusion: this mode is identical to the **Difference** mode but is more subtle.

Hue: this mode replaces the base colour by the blend colour. The brightness and saturation of the base colour are preserved.

Saturation: this mode replaces the saturation of the base colour with that of the blend colour. The hue and luminosity of the base colour remain unchanged.

Colour: this mode replaces the hue and saturation of the base colour with those of the blend colour. The base colour's luminosity stays the same.

Luminosity: this mode replaces the luminosity of the base colour by that of the blend colour. The hue and saturation of the base colour are preserved.

H-Inserting text into an image

Defining the type of text

Activate the 𝕋 tool.

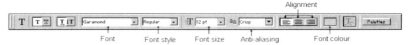

The options bar indicates the settings specific to text.

Select the type of text you wish to create by activating one of these buttons on the options bar:

T: to create a layer on which the text will be placed. This is a special layer which allows you to modify the text whenever you like, called a **type layer**. This is represented by a type layer thumbnail 𝕋 in the **Layers** palette.

: to create a selection whose outlines take the shape of a text. You can then fill this selection with a certain colour. This allows you to create text with a photographic background, as opposed to text filled with a solid colour.

Select the orientation of the text by clicking the button to create horizontal text or the button to create a vertical text.

Formatting characters

If the tool is not active, activate it.

Use the **Window - Show Character** command or click the **Palettes** button on the options bar then click the **Character** tab to see all the formatting options on the palette.

If you activated the button on the options bar, you can deactivate the **Rotate Characters** option in the **Character** palette menu (▶) to turn towards the right all the vertical letters or only the selected letters.

Select an **Anti-aliasing** method on the options bar to avoid a pixelation effect on the text outline. Choose **None** to keep a pixelated outline, **Crisp** to smooth the text outline without sacrificing too much quality, **Strong** to make a more obvious, almost bold text with a more blurred outline or **Smooth** to smooth the text without taking into account the text quality.

Deactivate the **Fractional Widths** option in the **Character** palette menu (▶) to remove varying character spacing (made in fractions of pixels); this can improve readability for text of less than 20 pixels in size.

Formatting paragraphs

If the tool is not active, activate it.

Use the **Window - Show Paragraph** command or click the **Palettes** button on the options bar then click the **Paragraph** tab to see all the formatting options on a palette.

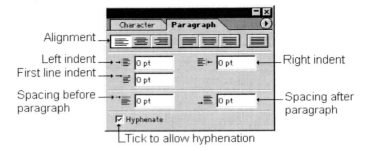

Alignment

Left indent
First line indent

Right indent

Spacing before paragraph

Spacing after paragraph

Tick to allow hyphenation

Inserting new text

▨ If the $\boxed{\text{T}}$ tool is not active, activate it.

▨ Depending on the type of text you want to create, perform one of these actions:

Click   to create point type. This has no limit, the paragraph length grows with the text but paragraph formatting is limited.

Drag   to create paragraph type. A bounding box cordons off the text:

> Paragraph text appears within a bounding box, complete with selection handles. If the text you type is too long in relation to the size of the box, a plus (+) sign appears in the bottom right corner. This is the case here, as

The bounding box can be resized, rotated or skewed (leaned to one side). The text wraps to the next line automatically when it reaches the right edge of the box.

▨ Enter your required text. As for standard text, you can press $\boxed{\text{Enter}}$ on the alphanumerical keyboard to change line or paragraph.

The text appears as you type.

▨ To confirm what you have typed, click the $\boxed{\checkmark}$ button on the options bar or press $\boxed{\text{Enter}}$ on the number pad or activate another tool. To cancel any undesired entry or text changes, use the $\boxed{\times}$ button on the options bar or press $\boxed{\text{Esc}}$.

⇨ *You can specify an exact size for the bounding box for paragraph text by holding down the $\boxed{\text{Alt}}$ (PC) or $\boxed{\text{⌐}}$ (Mac) key as you start to drag the bounding box. Give the required **Width** and **Height** and click **OK**.*

⇨ *Many menu commands become unavailable when the $\boxed{\text{T}}$ tool is active.*

I- Modifying text on a type layer

Modifying text or its formatting

▨ Double-click the thumbnail of the type layer on which your text is placed. Be careful to click the thumbnail and not the layer name, which will open the **Layer Style** dialog box instead of letting you modify the text.

The ⊞ *tool is activated automatically and the text is selected on the image.*

▨ To change the formatting, drag to select the text concerned then make the changes using the options in the **Character** and/or **Paragraph** palettes or on the options bar.

▨ To modify the text itself, click the text area, if necessary, and make the required changes.

▨ To confirm what you have typed, click the ☑ button on the options bar or press ⌞Enter⌟ on the number pad or activate another tool. To cancel any undesired entry or text changes, use the ☒ button on the options bar or press ⌞Esc⌟.

Modifying the text type

▨ In the **Layers** palette, activate the type layer you wish to modify. Do not edit the text with the ⊞ tool because the necessary commands for changing the type of text will become unavailable.

▨ If you wish to change the text orientation, use the **Layer - Type - Horizontal** or **Layer - Type - Vertical** command.

▨ To modify the type of text, use one of these commands:

Layer - Type - Convert To Point Text

This converts the selected paragraph text to point text. Any paragraph formatting specific to paragraph text is lost. Photoshop may display a warning message.
If the paragraph text does not appear in its entirety in the bounding box, the hidden text will be discarded permanently during the conversion. Photoshop will display another warning.

Layer - Type - Convert To Paragraph Text

This converts the selected point text to paragraph text. The bounding box adjusts itself to the text automatically.

⇨ *If you wanted to select text using the* ⊞ *option of the* ⊞ *tool and not a type layer, you can, as for any layer, select the non-transparent areas of the layer by holding down the* ⌞Ctrl⌟ *(PC) or* ⌞⇧*⌟ *(Mac) key and clicking the type layer thumbnail. However, you cannot convert a selection of text into a type layer.*

IMAGE MODIFICATION

Warping text

▨ Activate the type layer you wish to warp then use the **Layer - Type - Warp Text** command.

You can also click the 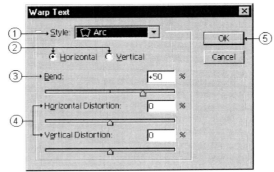 *tool on the options bar for the* **T** *tool.*

① Select the **Style** of text distortion you want to apply.

② Select the orientation for the warp effect. Depending on the type of warp you have chosen, these options could be unavailable or the effect may only really work with text oriented the same way.

③ Specify how marked the warp should be.

④ Change the value to give a perspective effect to the warped text.

⑤ Click to confirm.

The text is warped and the type layer thumbnail is modified, indicating that the text has been given a warp effect:

⇨ *You can modify an existing warp effect by proceeding as if you were warping the text for the first time. To remove a warp effect, modify it and in the* **Style** *list, select* **None**.

⇨ *You can apply other transformations to text using the* **Edit - Free Transform** *command or convert the text into image to apply further effects.*

⇨ *Warping is applied to the whole type layer. For paragraph text, the whole bounding box will be distorted.*

J- Using the paint bucket to change the colour of pixels

The *tool applies colour to a pixel and to its surrounding pixels, depending on how similar they are.*

▨ If necessary, activate the layer on which you wish to colour an area.

▨ Select a foreground colour as a fill colour or define a pattern then activate the ⬛ tool (which may be hidden by the ⬛ **Linear Gradient** tool).

① Use this list to choose whether you wish to fill with the **Foreground** colour or a **Pattern** if one has been defined.

② If necessary, adjust the blending mode and the opacity value for the fill.

③ Set a tolerance level between 0 and 255; if this is very low, only very similarly coloured pixels to the one you click will be filled.

④ Activate this option to avoid jagged edges on the outline of the filled area.

⑤ Activate this option to fill in the active layer with sampled colour taken from all layers present.

⑥ Leave this option active to fill only adjacent pixels.

▒ Click one of the pixels whose colour you want to modify.

K-Filling a selection with colour

▒ If necessary, select the colour that will be used for the fill then select the part of the image you want to paint.

▒ **Edit - Fill** or ⎡Û Shift⎤ ⎡←⎤

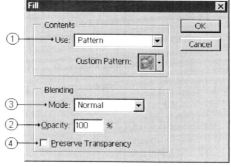

① Select the fill colour to use.

② Define the degree of transparency of the fill colour. The lower the value entered, the more the fill colour will be transparent.

③ Use this option to apply special fill effects, if required.

④ Activate this option if you do not want to fill in the transparent areas on a layer.

L-Filling a selection or a layer with a gradient

Using a preset gradient

▨ If necessary, activate the layer to which you want to apply the gradient or make a selection to limit the gradient.

▨ When working on a layer, activate the **Preserve Transparency** option if you want to limit applying the gradient just to the items on the layer.

▨ Activate this tool: [🔳].

① Select a predefined gradient in the gradient picker.

② Select the type of gradient by clicking one of these buttons.

③ Set the gradient's blending mode and opacity.

④ Tick this option to make the same gradient but with the colours reversed.

⑤ Tick this option to create gradients with less marked transitions.

⑥ Tick this option for gradients using a transparent colour. If this option is inactive, there will be no transparency in the gradient, except the transparency assigned with the **Opacity** option.

▨ Drag over the item to define the length of the gradient. You can use the ⎡⇧ Shift⎤ key if you want to make a horizontal or vertical gradient, or one that slopes at 45°.

⇨ *Within the gradient picker palette, there is a pop-up menu (⬤). This has options for modifying the appearance of the gradient picker but also enables you to load other gradients (the list appears at the bottom of the pop-up menu).*

Creating a custom solid gradient

▨ Activate the [🔳] tool.

▨ On the options bar, click the gradient sample at the left end of the bar to open the **Gradient Editor**.

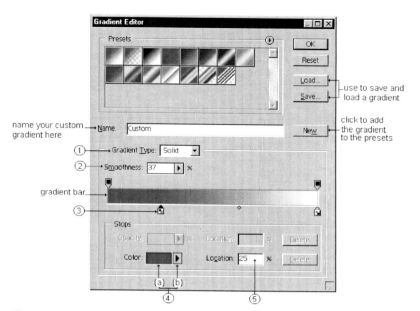

name your custom gradient here → **Name**

use to save and load a gradient

click to add the gradient to the presets

① ⟶ Gradient Type

② ⟶ Smoothness

gradient bar

③

Stops

④ (a) (b)

⑤

① Select **Solid** as the gradient type.

② Define the gradient's overall smoothness.

③ To modify a colour in the gradient, click the ⌂ symbol that corresponds (the tip of the symbol becomes black).

④ To select any colour, click the sample box (a). Click this button (b) to use the **Foreground Color** in the gradient; this is represented by the ⌂ symbol on the gradient bar. You can also use the background colour, represented by the ⌂ symbol. The **User Color** option is selected automatically if you click the **Color** sample box.

⑤ To set the transition distance between two colours in the gradient, enter a value. Between each ⌂ symbol, there is a mid-point (◇) which allows you to regulate at what point in the gradient the start and end colours will be evenly mixed. You can drag this mid-point to adjust it.

▓ To add a colour to the gradient, click under the gradient bar where the other color stops ⌂ are located and define the colour, by clicking in the sample box, for example.

▓ To delete a colour, drag the ⌂ symbol concerned downwards away from the bar or click the **Delete** button.

▓ To create or modify a gradient with transparency, proceed as for colour but use the ▽ symbols. Set the **Opacity** value and, if required, the **Location** of the gradient transparency.

As with colours, you can also add or remove transparencies or accumulate colour and transparency gradients.

IMAGE MODIFICATION

⇨ *You can **Rename Gradient** or **Delete Gradient** using these options in the pop-up menu (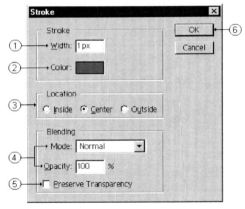) within the gradient picker. These commands are not available in the pop-up menu (●) within the **Gradient Editor** dialog box.*

⇨ *You can **Save Gradients** or **Load Gradients** using these options in the pop-up menu (●) within the gradient picker. Saved gradients are stored in the \Program Files\Adobe\Photoshop 6.0\Presets\Gradients folder by default. It is a good idea to use this folder as this will enable you to load the gradients from the pop-up menu (●) within the gradient picker or the pop-up menu (●) within the **Gradient Editor** dialog box.*

M- Adding stroke to a selection

▨ If necessary, select the colour you want to use for the outline (stroke).

▨ Select the part of the image that needs to have a stroked outline.

This is optional if you are going to apply stroke to all the images contained within one layer.

▨ **Edit - Stroke**

① Define the stroke width, which can attain a maximum of 16 pixels.

② If necessary, modify the stroke colour.

③ Determine where the stroke should be placed in relation to the selection's outline.

④ If required, select a blending mode and set the opacity.

⑤ Activate this option if the stroke is not to be applied to the transparent areas of a layer. On a layer, do not use this option when choosing an **Outside Location**.

⑥ Click to apply the stroke.

N-Creating a pattern

Select the area of the image that is going to be used to make the pattern. You can only select it with the  tool or by using **Select - All**.

Edit - Define Pattern

Enter the new pattern's **Name** and click **OK**.

O-Applying a pattern

Activate the layer on which you wish to use the pattern then activate the tool (it is in the same group as).

pop-up palette of brushes   pop-up palette of patterns

click to edit the brush

Select a **Brush** using the accompanying pop-up palette.

Set the **Opacity** and blending **Mode**.

Select the **Pattern** from the accompanying pop-up palette.

Leave the **Aligned** option active to avoid overlapping the tiles of pattern, using the same reference grid to apply the pattern. If this option is not active, you can overlap the pattern as you drag.

If you wish, you can **Fade** the brush **Size** and/or its **Opacity** with the options found by clicking the button on the options bar.

Drag over the area that you wish to fill with the pattern.

⇨ *You can also use **Edit - Fill** or ⟦⇧ Shift⟧ ⟦←⟧, selecting the **Pattern** option in the **Use** list.*

⇨ *You can also fill an image area with a pattern using the tool. On the options bar, choose **Pattern** under the **Fill** option then open the pop-up palette on the **Pattern** button to select a pattern. This method produces a less precise result than selecting an area and using the **Edit - Fill** command.*

⇨ *You can **Save Patterns** or **Load Patterns** using these options in the pop-up menu (⊙) that appears within the pop-up palette on the **Pattern** button. This appears in the options bar when the or tool is active or in the dialog box that appears with the **Edit - Fill** command. When saving patterns, you should use the \Program Files\Adobe\Photoshop 6.0\Presets\Patterns folder, as this will enable you to load the patterns from the pop-up menu (⊙). Patterns are kept during each work session but will only be memorised permanently if you save them. If you load other patterns, unsaved patterns will be lost permanently.*

P-Wrapping around the edges of a pattern or texture

▨ Create your pattern or texture in a new document.

▨ **Filter - Other - Offset**

This filter will show you how the edges of the pattern are joining up by moving the image and placing the removed pixels on the other side of the document.

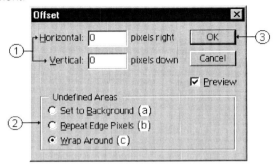

① Set the move distances. You can enter a value between -30 000 and +30 000.

② Determine how to fill the emptied spaces on the image:

    (a)   Fills the undefined areas with the background colour. If the offset is being made on a layer, the **Set to Transparent** option replaces this.

    (b)   The empty areas are filled by the remaining edge pixels.

    (c)   The areas of the image that were hidden by the moved portion now reappear on the opposite side of the picture.

③ Click to confirm.

The image moves and the edges are shifted around, which imitates the repetition of the image over a large area. If there is a continuity problem, a distinct cross can be perceived on the image. The cross effect should be corrected if you want to achieve a smooth tiling effect for the pattern or texture.

▨ Correct the image so the cross effect is no longer visible. To do this, use mainly the ⬛, ⬛, ⬛ and ⬛ tools.

▨ Check that the result is correct by making an offset in the opposite direction. If you used positive values in the first offset, use negative values and double them in relation to the first ones used (or vice versa). If the result is not correct, retouch again.

▨ If the cross effect can still be seen, correct it.

▨ Save the final result to keep your corrected texture or pattern.
If it is a texture, save it in **Photoshop (*.PSD, *.PDD)** format so you can re-use it with the **Texturizer** filter.

5.2 Copying and moving

A-Moving part of an image

- Select the part of the image or activate the layer containing the image you wish to move.

- Activate the ⊞ tool or press Ctrl (PC) or ⌘ (Mac) to use the tool temporarily.

- Point inside the selection and drag to the desired location (the pointer takes this form: ▶✥).

⇨ *Hold down* ⇧Shift *while dragging to obtain a horizontal, vertical or 45°* *movement. Use the arrow keys to move the image pixel by pixel. An* *arrow key plus* ⇧Shift *will move the image 10 pixels.*

B-Positioning part of an image with precision

- Select the part of the image or activate the layer to be moved.
- **Edit - Free Transform or** Ctrl **T**

- Select the reference point for the move by clicking the button representing the side of the selection on the options bar: ⊞.

- Activate the △ button to give a move value in relation to the selection's current position. Deactivate this button if you want to define the position of the selection in relation to the top left corner of the image.

- If the △ button is active, enter the horizontal move value in the **X** box and the vertical move value in the **Y** box. If the △ button is inactive, give the selection's horizontal and vertical position. You can also select the unit to use for **X** and **Y**.

- Press Enter to confirm the move or click the ✓ button on the options bar. To cancel, press Esc or click the ✕ button on the options bar.

C-Copying part of an image

- Select the part of the image or activate the layer to be copied.

- Activate the ⊞ tool or hold down Ctrl (PC) or ⌘ (Mac) to use the tool temporarily.

- Point inside the selection and hold down [Alt] (PC) or [⌥] (Mac) (the pointer will take this form: 🔲).
- Drag to the desired location, still holding down [Alt] (PC) or [⌥] (Mac).
- ⇨ *Copying is still a type of moving, so you can use the arrow keys as well as [⇧ Shift] to place the copy precisely.*
- ⇨ *You can also use the Windows clipboard to copy or move part of an image.*
- ⇨ *While the copy is still selected, you can move it with the 🔲 tool without a hole appearing on the image.*

D-Moving or copying onto a new layer

- If not already selected, select the part of the image as required.
- To move a selection, use **Layer - New - Layer Via Cut** or [Ctrl][⇧ Shift] **J**.
- To copy a selection, use **Layer - New - Layer Via Copy** or [Ctrl] **J**.

E-Copying layer effects or styles

- Activate the layer whose effects you want to copy.
- **Layer - Layer Style - Copy Layer Style**
- Activate the layer onto which you want to apply the copied effects then use **Layer - Layer Style**.
- Select the **Paste Layer Style** option to apply the effects only to this layer or the **Paste Layer Style to Linked** option to apply effects to all linked layers.
- ⇨ *When you copy a layer style, you copy the effects and also the layer blending options.*

F-Copying images located on several layers

- If necessary, mask all the layers whose contents are not to be copied then select the area of the image that you want to copy.
- **Edit - Copy Merged** or [Ctrl][⇧ Shift] **C** (PC) or [⌥ ⌘][⇧ Shift] **C** (Mac)
- Position the pointer or activate the destination layer.
- **Edit - Paste** or [Ctrl] **V** (PC) or [⌥ ⌘] **V** (Mac)

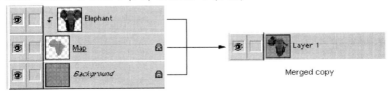

Merged copy

G-Copying or moving one selection into another

▦ Select the area of the image you want to copy then activate the **Edit - Copy** command (or ⌨ **C**) or **Edit - Cut** (or ⌨ **X**).

▦ Select the area in the image into which you want to paste the item you have just cut or copied.

▦ **Edit - Paste Into** or ⌨ ⇧ Shift **V** (PC) or ⌘ ⇧ Shift **V** (Mac)

The item is pasted onto a new layer, which is associated with a layer mask corresponding to the second selection.

⇨ *This command is especially useful if you wish to create specific effects on the layer mask or more particularly when working with images that do not accept layers, like **Indexed Color** or **Bitmap** mode images. For the latter, there will be no layer but there will be an equivalent result as long as you do not deselect.*

5.3 Transformations

A-Flipping/rotating an image

▦ Activate the layer or select the part of the image.

▦ **Edit - Transform**

▦ Choose the appropriate option for the transformation you wish to make.

⇨ *You can apply the same operation to the entire image (all layers included) by using the options found in **Image - Rotate Canvas**.*

B-Applying a precise transformation

▦ Activate the layer or select the part of the image.

▦ **Edit - Free Transform**

▦ Select the reference point for the transformation by clicking the button representing the side of the layer/selection on the options bar:

▦ To change the size of an object, enter a value in the **W** and **H** boxes to scale, respectively, the width and the height of the object. Activate the button if you want to keep the same proportions between the **Width** and the **Height**. You can use either percentages (%), cm, pt or px (pixels) as the unit.

▦ To skew (lean) an object, indicate in the **H** (horizontal) and **V** (vertical) boxes the required skew angle (between -89.99 and +89.99).

▦ If necessary, rotate the object on a certain angle by entering a value from -360 to 360 in the ⦣ zone on the options bar.

IMAGE MODIFICATION

Press ⌨Enter to confirm the transformation or click the ✅ button on the options bar. To cancel, press ⌨Esc or click the ❌ button on the options bar.

↪ *You can also make a precise rotation for the whole image (all layers included) by choosing **Image - Rotate Canvas - Arbitrary**.*

C-Applying other transformations

Free transformation allows you to apply five different transform options and to combine them: scale, rotate, skew, distort and perspective.

▨ Activate the layer or select part of the image.

▨ **Edit - Free Transform** or ⌨Ctrl **T** (PC) or ⌨⌘ **T** (Mac)
The selected image is surrounded by a bounding box, with selection handles. When the pointer appears inside this rectangle, it appears like this: ▶. You can then move the framed object.

▨ To rescale the object, point to one of the handles and drag. To keep the object's original proportions, hold down ⌨⇧Shift while dragging.

▨ To rotate the object, point outside the bounding border and drag. To force a 15°-angle rotation, hold down ⌨⇧Shift as you drag. To move the rotation centre represented by this symbol ✛, point to it and drag.

▨ To skew an object, hold down ⌨Ctrl⌨⇧Shift (PC) or ⌨⌘⌨⇧Shift (Mac) and drag one of the side handles. To make a symmetrical skew in relation to the centre of the bounding border, hold down ⌨Alt (PC) or ⌨⌥ (Mac) while you drag.

▨ To distort an object, which is a complete deformation in fact, hold down ⌨Ctrl (⌨⌘ on a Mac) and drag one of the handles. To make a symmetrical distortion in relation to the centre, hold down ⌨Alt (PC) or ⌨⌥ (Mac) while you drag.

▨ To apply a perspective effect, press ⌨Ctrl⌨Alt⌨⇧Shift (PC) or ⌨⌘⌨⌥⌨⇧Shift (Mac) and drag a corner handle.

▨ When the transformation(s) applied seem suitable, press ⌨Enter or click the ✅ button on the options bar. If not, press ⌨Esc or click ❌ on the options bar.

↪ *The whole point of the free transform options is that you can combine the various effects.*

↪ *You can also apply a transformation to a selection border using the **Select - Transform Selection** command.*

↪ *You can reproduce the last transformation you applied by using the **Edit - Transform - Again** command or pressing ⌨Ctrl⌨⇧Shift **T** (PC) or ⌨⌘ ⌨⇧Shift **T** (Mac).*

5.4 Filters

A-Applying a filter

Activate the layer on which you wish to apply a filter and, if necessary, select part of that layer if you need to limit its application.

Open the **Filter** menu and select a category then the filter you wish to use.

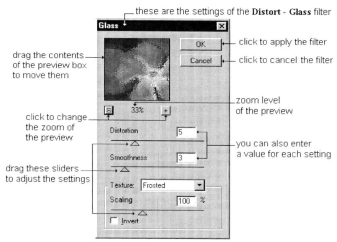

these are the settings of the **Distort** - **Glass** filter

drag the contents of the preview box to move them

click to apply the filter

click to cancel the filter

zoom level of the preview

click to change the zoom of the preview

you can also enter a value for each setting

drag these sliders to adjust the settings

⇨ You can interrupt the application of a filter by pressing [Esc].

⇨ You can reapply a filter using the same parameters by choosing the first command in the **Filter** menu (the name of this command corresponds to the last filter used) or by pressing [Ctrl] **F** (PC) or [⌘] **F** (Mac).

B-Softening the effect of a filter/adjustment or tool

After having applied a **Filter**, or made an adjustment with one of the **Image - Adjust** commands or used one of the drawing or retouching tools, use the command:

Filter - Fade [Name of filter, adjustment or tool] or [Ctrl][⇧ Shift] **F** (PC) or [⌘][⇧ Shift] **F** (Mac)

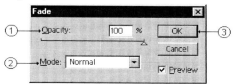

① Define the opacity to soften the effect's intensity.

② Select, if necessary, a blending mode to create an extra effect.

③ Click to fade the effect.

IMAGE MODIFICATION

C-Throwing light onto part of an image

*The **Lighting Effects** filter allows you to project various types of light onto an image. This filter only applies to RGB images.*

Filter - Render - Lighting Effects

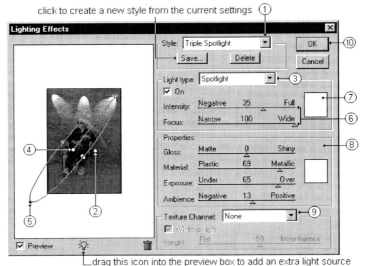

click to create a new style from the current settings ①

drag this icon into the preview box to add an extra light source

① If required, select a predefined style for the effect.

② If using several light sources, select the one you want to adjust.

③ Select a light type for the selected lighting effect.

④ Move the light source, if necessary.

⑤ Depending on the **Light type**, adjust the light source:

Directional

Drag point **(a)** to modify the angle and/or the distance of the light. Hold down ⇧ Shift to change direction without changing the angle. Hold down Ctrl (⌘ ⁎ on a Mac) to modify the angle without changing the distance.

Omni

Drag one of the four handles to modify the size of the light beam, as if the light bulb were moving closer or further away.

Spotlight

Drag point **(a)** to modify the light angle. Drag one of the four handles to modify the shape of the beam. Hold down ⇧ Shift to change the shape of the beam without changing its angle. Hold down Ctrl (PC) or ⌘ ⁎ (Mac) to modify the angle without changing the shape of the beam.

⑥ Set the intensity of the selected source, that is, its luminosity value. For **Spotlight** lights, set the width of the focus. This determines what quantity of light is emitted from the beam.

⑦ Change the colour of the light.

⑧ Define the properties of the selected light source.

⑨ If required, use a texture channel to modify the way in which the light is reflected. Activate the **White is high** option to increase the relief on light areas of the texture. Deactivate this option to accentuate the dark areas on the texture. Set the **Height** slider to accentuate or tone down the texture's relief.

⑩ Click to apply the filter.

⇨ *To delete a light, drag its central point from the preview screen to the* 🗑 *icon on the dialog box.*

D-Applying a texture to an image

▨ If necessary, activate the layer to which the texture will be applied or select something.

▨ **Filter - Texture - Texturizer**

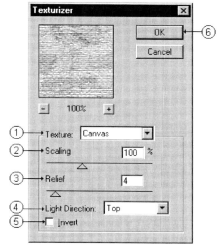

① Select the texture you wish to apply in the list or use the **Load Texture** option to open a PSD document.

② Change the size of the texture.

③ Determine the depth of the texture "engraved" on the image.

④ Specify how the texture should be lit.

⑤ This option reverses the lighting direction when active.

⑥ Click to apply the filter.

IMAGE MODIFICATION

E-Applying a 3D effect to an image

With this filter, you can treat a two-dimensional image as if it were a 3D image. 3D effects can only be applied to RGB images.

Activate the layer on which you wish to make the transformation.

Filter - Render - 3D Transform

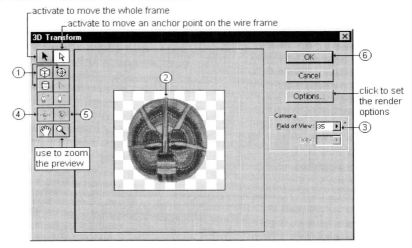

① Choose the type of 3D structure you wish to create (sphere, cube or cylinder).

② On the image in the preview box, drag to draw the structure (wire frame) for the selected shape.

③ Increase or reduce the wire frame.

④ Use this tool to move the wire frame and/or use the **Dolly** option to increase or decrease this area.

⑤ Use this tool to turn the outlined area on the 3D shape and/or use the **Dolly** option to increase or decrease this area.

⑥ Click to apply the filter.

⇨ *To delete a wire frame, select it with the* ![tool] *tool and press the* [Del] *key.*

A-Converting a colour image from one colour model to another

Converting an RGB or CMYK image into LAB

▦ If the image is in **16 Bits/Channel** convert it to **8 Bits/Channel** and if necessary, merge any adjustment layers so as not to lose their effects.

▦ **Image - Mode - Lab Color**

▦ If the image contains one or more layers, Photoshop will want to make certain changes during the conversion:

- If the image contains an adjustment layer, you may see this message:

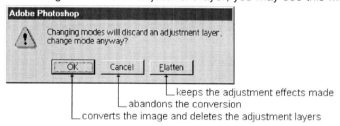

└ keeps the adjustment effects made
└ abandons the conversion
└ converts the image and deletes the adjustment layers

- If the image contains a normal layer, you may see this message:

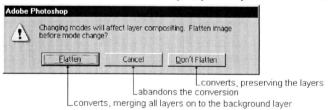

└ converts, preserving the layers
└ abandons the conversion
└ converts, merging all layers on to the background layer

⇨ *Images in Bitmap mode cannot be converted into Lab mode.*

⇨ *Use the **Image - Mode - RGB Color** command to convert a CMYK or Lab image to RGB.*

⇨ *To preview the converted image to see the result in several environments, use the **View - Proof Setup** command.*

Converting an RGB or LAB image into CMYK

▦ If the image is in **16 Bits/Channel**, you should switch to **8 Bits/Channel**.

▦ To make the most accurate conversion possible, by viewing the out-of-gamut colours beforehand, use **View - Gamut Warning** or ⌈Ctrl⌉⌈⇧ Shift⌉ **Y** (PC) or ⌈⌘ ⁂⌉ ⌈⇧ Shift⌉ **Y** (Mac).

This command determines which areas of the image will suffer colour loss during the conversion.

IMAGE MODIFICATION

- If considerable areas of the image appear as out-of-gamut, select these colours with **Select - Color Range**. Choose **Out Of Gamut** in the **Select** list and click **OK**.

- Create a feathered contour around the selection to avoid corrections that are too harsh, by using **Select - Feather**.

- Correct the saturation or even the hue slightly with a **Hue/Saturation** adjustment layer in the foreground, in front of all the other layers. To avoid harsh corrections, you may need to perform these last two steps several times. For more specific saturation retouches, use the ▣ tool with a low pressure.

- If necessary, merge the adjustment layers to preserve their effects then deactivate the display of non-printing colours with **View - Gamut Warning**.

- To preview the image as it will appear after conversion, use **View - Preview - CMYK** or ⟦Ctrl⟧ **Y** (PC) or ⟦⌘ ⟧ **Y** (Mac).

- If the colour distortion is too noticeable, deactivate the preview by repeating **View - Preview - CMYK** then make further corrections.

- If necessary, deactivate the preview with **View - Preview - CMYK** then make the conversion using **Image - Mode - CMYK Color**.

⇨ *You can convert CMYK images without constraint into Grayscale and Duotone. For Indexed Color images, you cannot check for out-of-gamut colours. In this case, make an initial conversion to RGB to check this.*

⇨ *You can change the colour used to highlight out-of-gamut colours with the* Edit - Preferences - Transparency & Gamut *command.*

B-Converting an image into grayscale

- If necessary, merge the adjustment layers to preserve their effects.

- **Image - Mode - Grayscale**

  *If the image contains no other layers than the **Background** layer, Photoshop prompts for confirmation before removing the colours.*

  If the image contains several layers, Photoshop offers to delete or merge any existing adjustment layers or to flatten or preserve any ordinary layers.

⇨ *If you are converting an image in Bitmap mode, Photoshop may ask for a size ratio to scale down the image. The higher this ratio, the smaller the image, but the number of shades of grey will be higher.*

⇨ *For a good quality conversion, prepare the image beforehand using the channel mixer.*

C-Converting a grayscale image to Bitmap

▧ Merge the adjustment layers before converting. Conversion cannot take place if adjustment layers are present in the document.

▧ **Image - Mode - Bitmap**

▧ If you have not flattened the image layers, you should do that now.

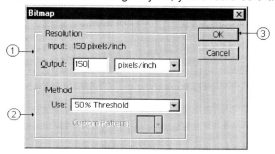

① Set the image resolution used, if required.

② Select the desired conversion method:

50% Threshold: all the pixels containing more than 50% black are converted to black and all the rest become white: this method produces a highly contrasted result.

Pattern Dither: simulates shades of grey by creating geometric shapes made up of black and white dots.

Diffusion Dither: simulates shades of grey by error-diffusion. The error margin is determined when the first pixel in the top left corner is converted.

Halftone Screen: simulates shades of grey by using halftone dots. These dots are linked to a screen, which functions in relation to the screen ruling, the screen angle and the dot shape used (these options concern more advanced printing techniques).

Custom Pattern: this method applies a texture to the screen, using the pattern defined with the **Edit - Define Pattern** command.

③ Click to convert.

▧ If you select the **Halftone Screen** option, define the screen then click **OK**.

⇨ *Only Grayscale and Multichannel images can be converted into Bitmap mode. If you convert a Multichannel image, only the active channel will be used and all others will be deleted.*

D-Converting an RGB image into Indexed Color

▨ If the image is in **16 Bits/Channel**, convert it to **8 Bits/Channel**.

▨ **Image - Mode - Indexed Color**

▨ Click **OK** if necessary to flatten the image and proceed with the conversion.

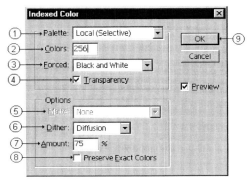

① Select the type of **Palette** that you wish to apply:

Exact: this option is available if the image does not contain more than 256 colours, in which case, it is offered by default. The image undergoes no changes and all the colours can be integrated into the colour table.

System (Mac OS) or **(Windows)**: uses the Macintosh or Windows system palette to make the conversion. If the image is to be used on a Macintosh or under Windows, you can use this option to ensure an optimum display in 256-colour mode.

Web: converts with a palette of 216 colours used by most Internet browsers to display 8 bit images.

Uniform: uses a palette based on a uniform colour sample of the image's whole colour spectrum. Photoshop takes between 2 and 6 levels for each of the red, green and blue components and combines them to make a uniform palette.

Perceptual: converts with a palette made up of the actual colours in the image, giving priority to colours to which the human eye is sensitive.

Selective: similar to the **Perceptual** option, this palette makes more use of large areas of colour and preserves Web colours.

Adaptive: similar to the **Perceptual** option, it converts using a palette made from the most common colours in the image, without giving priority to any particular colour.

Custom: this allows you to use a specific palette over several images, which can be useful for multimedia applications.

Previous: lets you apply the palette used to make the last conversion, providing it was made with a **Perceptual**, **Selective**, **Adaptive** or **Custom** palette.

② If you select a **Uniform**, **Perceptual**, **Selective** or **Adaptive** palette, you can define the number of colours used.

③ If you use a **Perceptual**, **Adaptive** or **Selective** palette, you can "force" certain colours into the palette.

④ Activate this option to preserve the transparent areas of the image. This option is only useful for images containing no **Background** layer.

⑤ Select the colour used to fill transparent areas.

⑥ If you use a different palette from **Exact**, select a dithering option to simulate the colours that do not appear in the palette.

⑦ If you use **Diffusion** dithering, set the density.

⑧ If you use **Diffusion** dithering choose this option to ensure dithering does not occur on colours which perfectly match those present in the original image.

⑨ Click to make the conversion.

E-Converting an image to duotone

▒ If the image is not in grayscale, convert it using **Image - Mode - Grayscale**.

▒ **Image - Mode - Duotone**

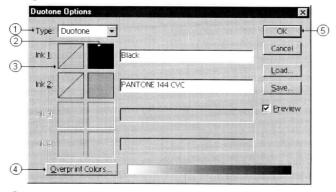

① Select the desired type of image, depending on how many inks you wish to use.

② Depending on what **Type** was chosen, click the different colour samples to specify what colour inks to use.

IMAGE MODIFICATION

③ Set the duotone curves to adjust the density of ink used:

enter the required density value
to add a point or remove the value
to erase the point

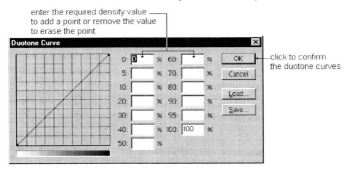

click to confirm
the duotone curves

④ Click this button to adjust the screen display in order to simulate the printed result correctly.

⑤ Convert the image.

F-Changing the size and/or resolution of an image

Image - Image Size

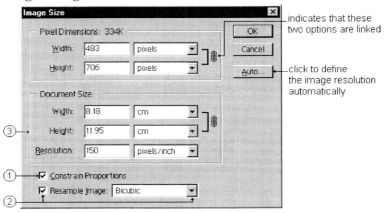

indicates that these two options are linked

click to define the image resolution automatically

① Leave this option active to adjust the **Height** automatically when you change the **Width** and vice versa.

② Leave the **Resample Image** option active if you wish to allow Photoshop to add or subtract pixels then indicate the interpolation method to be used: **Nearest Neighbor**, **Bilinear** or **Bicubic**.

③ Give the new width, height or resolution you require.

➪ *The default **Interpolation** method for the **Resample Image** option can be set in the **Edit - Preferences - General** dialog box.*

➪ *To make a quick check on an image's size and resolution, [Alt]-click (PC) or [⌐]-click (Mac) the position on the status bar where the document size is listed in Kb or Mb.*

G-Cropping an image

▨ Activate the  tool.

▨ Determine the **Width**, **Height** and **Resolution** of the image once it has been cropped. You can also click the **Front Image** button to use the **Width**, **Height** and **Resolution** of the current image automatically: the cropped image will then have the same values.

deletes the values indicated ⎯⎦

▨ If you want to see more information during cropping, show the **Info** palette.

▨ Drag a marquee around the image area that you want to keep.

A marquee (rectangle) with selection handles appears and the area that will be cut off darkens. Once you define a crop area, the options bar changes:

deactivate to remove the highlight
colour from the area that will be cut off

click to confirm the crop⌍
click to cancel it⌏

① If necessary, change the **Color** and **Opacity** used for the colour that highlights the area that will be cropped.

② Select the cropping mode to use on images with layers:

(a)   to delete layer areas located outside the crop marquee.

(b)   to hide all layer areas outside the crop marquee without deleting them. If you move a layer after cropping, the hidden areas will be displayed as usual.

③ Tick this option to distort the cropped image. Once you have ticked it, drag the corner handles of the crop marquee. The mouse pointer should take this form: ▶ .

You can also move the distortion axis by dragging the ⌖ symbol, located by default in the centre of the image. The result may differ markedly, depending on the position of this axis.

▨ You can rotate the crop marquee by placing the mouse pointer outside the crop marquee and dragging. You can also move the rotation axis by dragging the ⌖ symbol, located by default in the centre of the image. Hold down ⌗Shift while you drag to rotate to a 15° angle.

⇨ *You can also crop an image from a selection made with the* ⬚ *tool. Once the selection is made, activate the* **Image - Crop** *command.*

H-Scanning an image

If you have a scanner driven by an application managing the TWAIN interface, you can scan images in that application directly from Photoshop.

Place the document you wish to scan in the scanner then use:

File - Import - (name of scan application)

Before adjusting the various scan parameters, make a preview scan by clicking the button usually called **Preview**.

If the image you are scanning is smaller than the scan area, reduce the area, or in the opposite case, enlarge it.

Select an input **Resolution**.

Set the scanning mode. Most plug-ins allow you to choose from RGB mode, grayscale and black and white (or Bitmap). With a top-of-the-range scanner, you can also digitise directly in CMYK.

Most scanner plug-ins have settings optimised for certain types of documents. Select the document type from the list offered (the option names are given as examples: they will vary between different types of equipment):

A black and white drawing	Select the **Line Art** or **Black and White** option.
A colour drawing	Select **Coloured Art** or **Colour Drawing**. If a similar option is not offered, choose **Colour Photo**.
A black and white photo	Select the **Grayscale Photo** or **Black and White Photo** or **Grayscale** option.
A colour photo	Select the **Colour Photo** option.
A text document	Select the **Text** or **Line Drawing** or **Black and White** option.

If necessary, adjust the **Brightness** and/or **Contrast** settings.

If necessary, adjust the **Range** for grayscales.

If the scanning application has retouch functions, similar to the **Levels** and **Curves** commands in Photoshop, adjust these settings for optimal image quality.

When the settings appear correct, click the **Scan** button to scan and digitise the image.

When the image is digitised, it appears in a new window in Photoshop.

Quit the scan application to return to Photoshop and work on the image as required.

I- Extracting the foreground of an image

Activate the layer containing the detail to extract.

Image - Extract or ⌈Ctrl⌉⌈Alt⌉ **X** (PC) or ⌈⇧ ⌘⌋ ⌈⌐⌋ **X** (Mac)

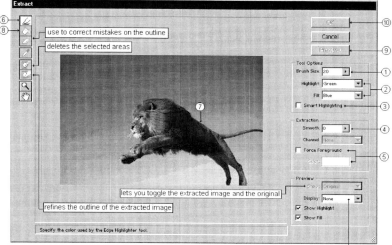

use to check the quality of the extraction by displaying it ⅃
on a coloured background or as a mask

① Specify the width of the edge highlighter.

② If necessary, change the highlight and fill colours.

③ To optimize the selection, tick this option to use minimal highlighting on the outline.

④ Modify this option to remove stray background pixels from the selection.

⑤ Activate this option if the background does not contrast well (especially if it is solid colour). Click the **Color** box and choose the colour to use for highlighting the selection or activate the 🖊 tool and click the colour in the preview area.

⑥ Activate this tool to outline your selection.

⑦ Point to the edge of the object and drag to outline it. If you have activated the **Force Foreground** option, you should also fill in the outline with the 🖊 tool.

⑧ If the **Force Foreground** option is not active, activate this tool to define the area of the foreground to extract, then click inside the outline.

⑨ Check the results of the extraction: parts of the image being discarded appear transparent.

⑩ Click to make the extraction.

⇨ *If the edges still need sharpening a little, you can use one of the following tools:* △, 🖌 *or* 🖌.

IMAGE MODIFICATION

J- Clipping an image

Before exporting an image to a desktop publishing application such as QuarkXPress, or a graphics application such as Illustrator, you should clip the image so the image background does not appear in the destination document.

▓ Activate the path that will be used to make the clipping path. This must be a saved path.

▓ Activate the **Clipping Path** command on the **Paths** palette menu (⬤).

▓ Select the **Path** that outlines the object.

▓ Specify how precisely the path's curves are reproduced with the **Flatness** option (from 0.2 to 100).

▓ Click **OK** to confirm.

▓ In the **Paths** palette, the path used for the clipping path is indicated in bold type.

▓ If you wish to print the image, you may have to convert it to CMYK.

▓ Save the image in **Photoshop EPS** format. If you convert to CMYK mode, you can also use **Photoshop DCS 1.0** and **Photoshop DCS 2.0** formats.

The document is saved and can be imported into a desktop publishing application.

K-Adding/deleting annotations on an image

▓ Create or open the file in .PDF or .PSD format to which you wish to add notes, then activate the 🖽 tool to add a written note to the image or the 🔊 tool to add a voice note (for this you will need a microphone).

▓ Complete the fields shown in the options bar (**Author, Font** etc.).

▓ Click the place on the image where you wish to place the annotation.

▓ If you are using the 🔊 tool, click the **Start** button (**Record** on a Mac) to start recording the note then the **Stop** button when you have finished.

If you are using the 🖽 tool, enter the note text in the special window that opens.

▓ To read the note, or listen to it, double-click the note symbols on the image as follows: 🗍 or ◁ .

▓ You can move the note by dragging this symbol on the image.

⇨ *To delete notes, activate the* 🖼️ *or* 🔊 *tool, click the **Clear All** button on the options bar and click **OK**.*

L- Cutting an image into slices

This is an especially useful function when you are creating Web images. The image will download in several pieces, which tends to make the Internet user less impatient than if he or she has to look at an empty space while a picture downloads. You can also set links to different slices of the image.

▒ Activate the 🖊️ tool.

① Select the style for defining the slice.

② Leave this option active to see in which order the different image slices will be saved.

③ Select the line colour that will be used to highlight the slice marks on the image.

▒ Drag on the image to make a slice.

*The slices are marked by an outline, whose colour is defined in the **Line Color** option on the options bar, and each slice has an order number.*

⇨ *To hide or display the slices on a image, use the **View - Show - Slices** command.*

M- Modifying or deleting a slice

▒ Activate the 🖊️ tool.

▒ Click the slide that you wish to edit or delete.

▒ If you want to resize it, but no resizing handle appears around the slice, click the **Promote To User Slice** button on the options bar.

▒ Drag one of the handles around the edge of the slice to resize it. If you reduce its size, one or more additional slices will be created.

▒ Modify the stacking order of overlapping slices by clicking one of these buttons on the options bar:

 to put the current slice into the foreground/background.

 to place the current slice forward/backward one level.

▒ Press ⌨️Del or ⌨️← to delete a slice.

N-Setting slice options

░ Activate the 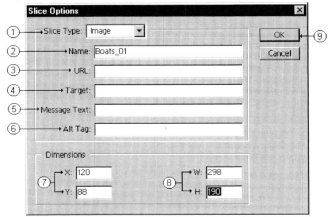 tool.

░ Click the slice whose options you want to modify then click the **Slice Options** button on the options bar or double-click the slice.

① Define the type of slice in the corresponding box:

No Image: no image will be visible on this slice. Enter the text that should be displayed instead of the image in the **HTML** text box. To view the result, activate the **File - Save for Web** command and click the **Preview in browser** button (this button has the icon of your Web browser on it).

Image: the image will be displayed normally and you can assign a link to it.

② If you chose an **Image** slice type, define the name of the image that will be created when saved with the **File - Save for Web** command.

③ Define a hyperlink towards another Internet page by entering the **URL**.

④ If required, define where the page given in the **URL** box will be displayed, by entering one of these elements:

_blank: shows the linked page in a new browser window.

_self: shows the linked page in the same frame as the current HTML page.

_parent: shows the linked page in its original frame. Use this option if the current image is a child of this frame.

_top: shows the linked page in the current browser window by replacing all its contents.

⑤ Define the message that will appear in the browser's status bar when you point to a slice. By default, the **URL** is displayed.

⑥ Define the text that will replace the image in non-graphical browsers.

⑦ If required, define in pixels the precise position of the slice.

⑧ If required, set the precise size of the slice in pixels, to define its width and height respectively.

⑨ Click to confirm.

5.6 Image retouching

A-Distorting an image

▨ **Image - Liquify** or Ctrl ⇧Shift **X** (PC) or ⌘ * ⇧Shift **X** (Mac)

▨ In the **Liquify** dialog box, set the **Brush Size** for the distortion tool in the appropriate box.

▨ Set the **Brush Pressure** the tool will exert, using the corresponding text box.

▨ If you are using a pressure-sensitive graphics tablet, activate the **Stylus Pressure** option to use the pressure exerted on the tablet.

▨ Distort the image by activating one of these tools:

 to push the pixels when you drag the tool over the image.

 to make the pixels rotate when you hold the mouse button down over the image. The rotation occurs in a clockwise direction.

 to produce the same effect as with the ⟨image⟩ tool but in the opposite direction.

 to contract the pixels towards the centre of the tool (or push them out from the centre) when you hold the mouse button down over the image.

 to move the pixels vertically or horizontally when you drag over the image.

 to copy the pixels located outside the brush form to the inside of the brush form.

▨ Drag or hold the mouse button down over an area of the image to make the distortion.

⇨ *Tick the Show Mesh option to see a fine grid over the image. This will be distorted at the same time as the image, giving you a better appreciation of the distortion as it is applied. Define how fine this mesh should be with the Mesh Size option and change its colour with the Mesh Color option.*

B-Freezing/thawing areas of an image

▓ Open the **Liquify** dialog box.

▓ Freeze certain parts of the image so they are not distorted or modified:

    – using the  tool: you can drag over the image areas you want to protect.

    – using an alpha channel: in this case, select the alpha **Channel** from this list in the **Freeze Area** frame.

▓ If you wish, click the **Invert** button in the **Freeze Area** frame to make the frozen areas the unprotected areas and vice versa.

▓ Thaw (or unfreeze) the frozen areas by activating the tool and dragging over the image. You can also thaw all the frozen areas by clicking the **Thaw All** button in the **Freeze Area** frame.

⇨ *To modify the colour of frozen areas, use the **Freeze Color** option.*

⇨ *Deactivate the **Show Frozen Areas** option if you do not want the frozen areas to be highlighted with a specific colour.*

C-Reconstructing an image

▓ Open the **Liquify** dialog box and activate **Revert** in the **Mode** list, under **Reconstruction**.

▓ Activate the tool.

▓ Drag over the area of the image on which you would like to revert to the original image.

▓ Click the **Reconstruct** button to put all the unfrozen areas back to their original state.

▓ Click the **Revert** button to revert to the original including for the frozen areas.

D-Duplicating part of an image with the rubber stamp

The rubber stamp paints with a sampled area of an image rather than with any individual colour.

▓ If your image contains several layers, activate the layer which will act as the reference for this duplication. You can also open another image if you want to reproduce an area from that image.

▓ Activate the tool.

① Choose a blending mode for the tool and an opacity level.

② Activate this option to reproduce an area of the image without taking into account which layer is active.

③ Leave this option active to apply the sampled area as a whole, whether or not you stop and start your painting. If the option is deactivated, the duplication will begin again from the initial sampling point each time you stop dragging then start again.

④ Select a brush type from the pop-up palette.

⑤ Click this button and select the **Fade** option for the **Size** and/or **Opacity** options so the tool fades to zero brush size or to transparency.

▨ Indicate the initial sampling point by pointing to the area you want to reproduce. Hold down [Alt] (PC) or [⌘] (Mac) and click.

▨ Point to the area you want to retouch and drag to start painting.

Two pointers appear on the screen: the cross hair indicates the part of the image that is being reproduced and the second pointer shows the tool as it is being used.

E-Creating flat areas of colour

▨ If necessary, activate a layer or make a selection.

▨ **Image - Adjust - Posterize**

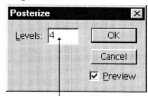

```
specify the number of the brightness levels
for each colour channel (between 2 and 255)
```

The image now looks more like a drawing than a photo.

F-Using the Smudge tool

Imagine that your photo has been painted and the paint is still wet. The Smudge tool produces an effect similar to spreading wet paint with your finger.

▨ If necessary, activate the layer on which you want to work.

▨ Activate the ![tool] tool (in the same tool group as the ![tool] tool).

① Select the blending mode you want to use then define the tool's pressure.

② Activate this option to spread a colour featured on another layer than the active one.

③ Activate this option if you wish to spread the foreground colour as opposed to the colours on the image.

④ Open the pop-up palette of brushes and choose your tool size.

⑤ Click this button and select the **Fade** option for the **Size** and/or **Pressure** options so the tool fades to zero brush size or to a weak effect.

▨ Drag over the area whose colours you wish to spread out.

G-Blurring or sharpening part of an image

▨ If necessary, activate the layer you want to work on.

▨ Activate the ⬡ tool to blur the chosen area or the ⬡ tool to obtain a greater contrast over the chosen area.

▨ In the options bar, select the blending mode for the tool and adjust the **Pressure** you want to exert on the image.

▨ Activate the **Use All Layers** option if you want the tools to blur or sharpen using data from all visible layers.

▨ Open the pop-up palette on the **Brush** option and select a brush type.

▨ Click the ⬚ button on the options bar and select the **Fade** option for the **Size** and/or **Pressure** options so the tool fades to zero brush size or to a weak effect.

▨ Drag over the area that should be more blurred or sharper. You can press ⬚ (PC) or ⬚ (Mac) to switch momentarily to the ⬡ tool from the ⬡ tool, and vice versa.

⇨ *To blur or sharpen large areas of an image, it may be better to use selections and/or layers in conjunction with the Filter - Blur - Blur/Blur More/Gaussian Blur command or with the Filter - Sharpen/Sharpen Edges/Sharpen More command.*

H-Darkening or lightening part of an image

▨ If necessary, activate the layer on which you want to work.

▨ Activate the ⬚ tool to lighten an area of the image or the ⬚ tool to darken an area of the image.

▨ Using the **Range** option on the options bar, choose to which type of tones the retouch should apply: **Shadows** to work on dark parts of the image, **Midtones** to change the luminosity over most areas of the image or **Highlights** to work on light tones.

▨ In the **Exposure** list, give a value to determine how quickly the tool will lighten or darken the image.

▨ Open the pop-up palette of brushes and choose your tool size.

- Click the ▨ button on the options bar and select the **Fade** option for the **Size** and/or **Pressure** options so the tool fades to zero brush size or to a weak effect.

- Drag over the area that should be lightened or darkened. You can press ⌈Alt⌉ (PC) ⌈⌐⌐⌋ (Mac) if you wish to switch briefly from the ▨ tool to the ▨ tool and vice versa.

⇨ *You can use the **Image - Adjust - Equalize** command to modify an image's contrast and brightness automatically. For images with a strong light or dark dominant, this can result in an improved distribution of luminosity.*

I- Modifying colour saturation on an area of an image

- Activate, if necessary, the layer where the retouch is to be made.

- Activate the ▨ tool, which is in the same tool group as the ▨ and ▨ tools.

- On the options bar, select the blending **Mode** for the tool, **Desaturate** to dull the colour or **Saturate** to give more brilliance to a colour.

- Set the **Pressure** to determine how quickly the tool will saturate or desaturate the image.

- Open the pop-up palette of brushes and choose your tool size.

- Click the ▨ button on the options bar and select the **Fade** option for the **Size** and/or **Pressure** options so the tool fades to zero brush size or to a weak effect.

- Drag over the part of the image you want to modify.

5.7 Colour correction

A-Managing an image's colour table

When you change the mode of an image to indexed color, Photoshop creates a colour table which brings together a number of colours, limited to 256 colours.

- **Image - Mode - Color Table**

Table: Custom ▾

OK

Cancel

Load...

Save...

☑ Preview

use to open
a saved table

click to open
a saved table

click to save
these settings
to use them
with another image

click a colour
with this tool
to make it
transparent

click to modify
a colour

drag from a start to an end colour to create a gradient

B-Using the Color Sampler tool

This tool supplies you with vital information about the colour components of four points on the image.

▨ Activate the ▨ tool.

▨ Click an area on the image to define the first sample and as required, define three other samples.

*The information concerning the samples appears in the **Info** palette.*

▨ If needed, move the sample points by dragging them.

▨ To delete a sample point, hold down Alt (PC) or ⌐ (Mac) and click the point.

C-Checking the tonal range of a picture

*The aim of analysing an image with a histogram is to tell whether a digital image has a dark or light dominant (its **tonal range**) so that you can see which corrections in tone need to be made.*

▨ For a document made of several layers, hide all the layers except the one that you wish to check.

▨ **Image - Histogram**

▨ You can make an overall analysis of the picture using the **Luminosity** option or by each channel of colour to trace any colour dominants.

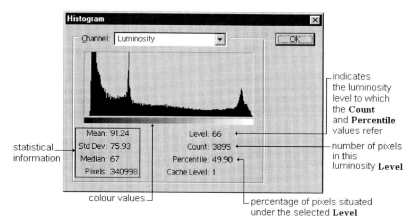

indicates the luminosity level to which the Count and Percentile values refer

number of pixels in this luminosity Level

statistical information

Mean: 91.24	Level: 66
Std Dev: 75.93	Count: 3895
Median: 67	Percentile: 49.90
Pixels: 340998	Cache Level: 1

colour values

percentage of pixels situated under the selected Level

With a poor quality image, you will obtain a histogram with large gaps and a low number of pixels.

▦ To ensure a good quality image, check its black point by pointing to the left edge of the histogram: if the value which appears in **Level** is greater than 10, the image lacks detail in its dark areas.

▦ Next, check its white point by pointing to the right edge of the histogram. If the **Level** value is less than 240, detail is poor in the light areas of the image.

▦ Click **OK**.

⇨ *The histogram is not always completely accurate. To confirm the black point and white point readings, use the Image - Adjust - Levels command.*

D-Adjusting the proportions of colour in an image

Using the simplified method

▦ If necessary, activate the layer on which you wish to work or select an area of the image to limit your retouching.

▦ **Image - Adjust - Variations**

IMAGE MODIFICATION

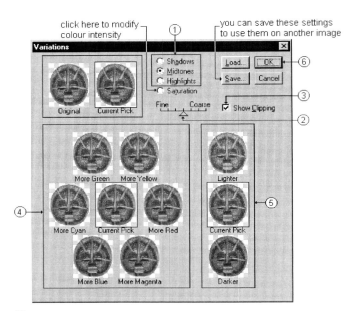

① Select the tones with which you want to work.

② Change the speed of the adjustment by moving the slider.

③ Leave this option active to display in a bright colour the pixels that will become black or white (depending on whether the active option is **Shadows** or **Highlights**). If the **Saturation** option is being used, the **Show Clipping** option allows you to see if any pixels exceed the maximum saturation.

④ To adjust the colour proportions, click one of these variations.

⑤ Click one of the variations to modify the image brightness. Each time you click a variation, both **Current Pick** areas consequently change: the **Original** preview allows you to compare the picture before and after retouching.

⑥ Click to confirm.

By adjusting the colour balance

☷ If necessary, activate the layer on which you wish to work or select an area of the image to limit the adjustment to that area.

☷ **Image - Adjust - Color Balance** or Ctrl **B** (PC) or ⌂⌘ **B** (Mac)

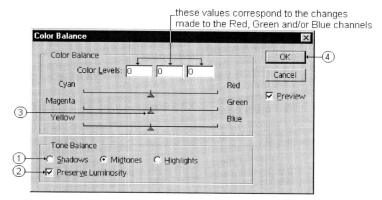

these values correspond to the changes
made to the Red, Green and/or Blue channels

① Select the tone with which you want to work.

② With an image in RGB, leave this option active to preserve the harmony between dark, light and midtones, without changing the image brightness.

③ Drag a slider to increase the proportion of a specific colour in the chosen image or layer.

④ Click to confirm.

By changing the histogram or the curves

▒ If necessary, activate the layer on which you want to work or select an area of the image to limit the adjustment to that area.

▒ To adjust the histogram, use **Image** - **Adjust** - **Levels** or <kbd>Ctrl</kbd> **L** (PC) or <kbd>⌘ ⌦</kbd> **L** (Mac). To adjust using the curves, use **Image** - **Adjust** - **Curves** or <kbd>Ctrl</kbd> **M** (PC) or <kbd>⌘ ⌦</kbd> **M** (Mac).

▒ To modify an image's colours, use the **Channel** option on the various dialog boxes (**Levels** or **Curves**) and adjust each channel on the image or layer.

▒ Click **OK**.

⇨ These last two methods are the more precise. Avoid other methods when you require a high quality result.

IMAGE MODIFICATION

E-Adjusting individual colour components

By modifying the hue or saturation

▓ Image - Adjust - Hue/Saturation or [Ctrl] U (PC) or [⌂ ⌘] U (Mac)

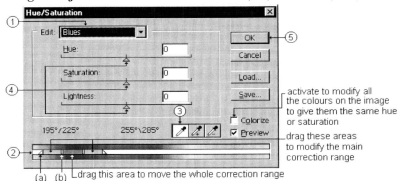

drag these areas to modify the main correction range

activate to modify all the colours on the image to give them the same hue or saturation

(a) (b) └drag this area to move the whole correction range

① Select the hue that you want to correct, if you have chosen to work on another hue than **Master**. The triangular sliders **(a)** cordon off the total correction range. The rectangular sliders **(b)** show the main correction range corresponding to the selected colour.

② If necessary, drag sliders (a) and (b) to extend or compress the correction range.

③ If you are working on a colour other than **Master**, activate this tool this click on the part of the image that contains the colour you want to modify.

④ Make your corrections. Drag the **Hue** slider to modify the colours. Drag the **Saturation** slider to modify the brilliance of colours, much as with the [▓] tool, but in an overall way on the image, layer, selection or chosen colour. Drag the **Lightness** slider to modify the brightness with the same method used by the **Image - Adjust - Brightness/Contrast** command.

⑤ Click to confirm.

⇨ *To desaturate a picture rapidly, you can use the* **Image - Adjust - Desaturate** *or press* [Ctrl][⇧ Shift] U *(PC) or* [⌂ ⌘] [⇧ Shift] U *(Mac). This will "grey out" all the colours.*

Using Selective Color

▓ If necessary, activate the layer you wish to retouch or select an area to limit the effects.

▓ **Image - Adjust - Selective Color**

▓ Select the **Colors** you wish to correct.

▓ Activate **Relative** if you want to keep the current colour proportions for each different hue or **Absolute** if you want to change the hues without taking the colour proportions into account.

▨ Drag the various sliders or enter a value of between -100 and +100 in the corresponding text boxes.

▨ Click **OK** to confirm.

▨ Click **Save** to save the settings you have defined.

▷ *This technique can also be used to remove a colour dominant. To do this, select the colour with the corresponding option and adjust the components.*

F-Replacing particular colours on an image

▨ If necessary, select the layer that you want to retouch.

▨ **Image - Adjust - Replace Color**

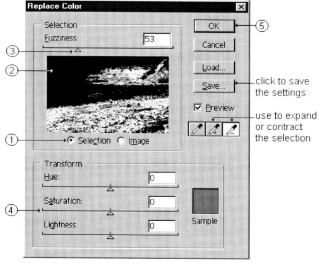

① To make your selection, use the **Selection** option to view the parts of the image that will be modified in the form of a mask or the **Image** option to view a thumbnail of the entire picture in the dialog box.

② Select the colour you want to modify by using the ⬚ tool in the dialog box then clicking the area that corresponds to the chosen colour on the image or on the preview screen in the dialog box.

③ Vary this option so it takes into account more or less similar shades.

④ Select the new colour with the sliders or enter values in the corresponding text boxes.

⑤ Click to modify the colours.

G-Adjusting contrast and/or brightness on an image

*The simplest method is to use the **Image - Adjust - Brightness/Contrast** command. If you require a more precise result, use the techniques described below.*

By modifying the histogram

▨ If necessary, activate the layer on which you need to work.

▨ **Image - Adjust - Levels** or ⌨Ctrl **L** (PC) or ⌨⌘ **L** (Mac)

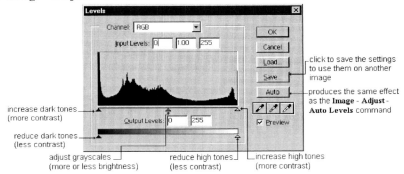

Using automatic levels or auto contrast

▨ If necessary, activate the layer you wish to retouch.

▨ Reset the auto levels if necessary: use the command **Image - Adjust - Levels** or **Image - Adjust - Curves**. Hold down the ⌨Alt key (PC) (⌨⌥ on a Mac)(the **Auto** button changes into an **Options** button) and click this **Options** button.

▨ Set the **Black Clip** and **White Clip** values between 0.01 and 9.99% then click **OK**.

▨ Click the **Cancel** button on the **Levels** or **Curves** dialog box.

▨ **Image - Adjust - Auto Levels** or ⌨Ctrl ⌨⇧Shift **L** (PC) or ⌨⌘ ⌨⇧Shift **L** (Mac)
Image - Adjust - Auto Contrast or ⌨Ctrl ⌨Alt ⌨⇧Shift **L** (PC) or ⌨⌘ ⌨⌥ ⌨⇧Shift **L** (Mac)

⇨ *To make an automatic adjustment on the brightness as well as the contrast, you can also use the **Image - Adjust - Equalize** command.*

By adjusting the curves

▨ If it is not already active, activate the layer on which you want to work.

▨ **Image - Adjust - Curves** or ⌨Ctrl **M** (PC) or ⌨⌘ **M** (Mac)

*The horizontal axis represents the original pixel values (**Input** values), and the vertical axis represents the new values (**Output** values). At the outset, the diagonal line is straight.*

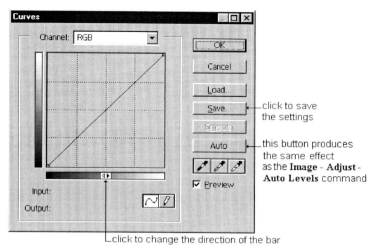

—click to save
the settings

—this button produces
the same effect
as the **Image - Adjust -
Auto Levels** command

—click to change the direction of the bar

▓ Before making any corrections, check that the luminosity bar looks like this: [ ] if you are working with an image in RGB; or like this: [ ] for an image in CMYK, Lab or grayscale.

▓ To define a curve, use the buttons:

 To define an even curve from selected points along it. To add a point, click along the curve or point to the area on the image you wish to correct and `Ctrl`-click (`⌘`-click on a Mac): the input point corresponding to the pixel you have clicked will be created on the curve. You can adjust the points created by dragging them. You can add to 14 points in this way.

 To draw a curve manually by dragging it or by using `⇧Shift`-clicks to draw straight lines. You can click the **Smooth** button to smooth out the new curve.

▓ When you add a point, the **Input** and **Output** values are indicated. Instead of changing the curve by dragging, you can add specific values.

▓ To delete a fixed point, drag it out of the curve area, or click to select it and press `Del`.

▓ Click **OK**.

⇨ *You can also hold down the* `Ctrl``⇧Shift` *keys (PC) or* `⌘``⇧Shift` *(Mac) and click the image to fix a point, not on its composite channel but on the curves of all the colour component channels.*

Using the black point and white point of an image

▓ If necessary, activate the layer on which you will be working then show the **Info** palette.

▓ **Image - Adjust - Levels** or **Curves** or `Ctrl` **L** or `Ctrl` **M** (PC) or `⌘` **L** or `⌘` **M** (Mac)

IMAGE MODIFICATION

Select the 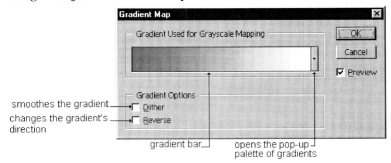 tool in the dialog box and click an area on the image or layer that corresponds to the darkest tones.

Select the tool in the dialog box then click on the lightest part of the image.

Click **OK**.

⇨ *You can modify the preferences of the tool to define the black and white points from the average values and not from the values of the most extreme pixels (the **Point Sample**). To do this, activate the tool and modify the **Sample Size** on the options bar before proceeding.*

⇨ *You can define the black and white points at a certain value by double-clicking the tool and/or the tool.*

⇨ *The **Image - Adjust - Equalize** command can be used to modify an image's contrast and brightness automatically. On images with a noticeable light or dark dominant, this can ensure a more homogenous distribution of luminosity.*

H-Replacing image colours or grayscales with a gradient

If your image is in grayscale, convert it to RGB, CMYK or Lab. If the image is in colour, its equivalent grayscale range will be used during the gradient fill.

If required, make a selection or activate a layer to limit the effect to that part of the image.

Image - Adjust - Gradient Map

smoothes the gradient
changes the gradient's direction
gradient bar
opens the pop-up palette of gradients

Select the gradient you wish to use or create it. The dark tones correspond to one extremity of the gradient and the light tones to the other extremity.

INDEX

INDEX

G

H

I

ILLUSTRATOR

IMAGE

IMPORTING

INDEXED COLOR

INFO

J

JPEG

L

LAB

LAYER

LAYER CLIPPING PATH

LAYER MASK

LAYER SET

INDEX

INDEX

S

SATURATION

SAVING

SCALING

SCANNING

SELECTING

See also SELECTION, TOOL

SELECTION

See also SELECTING

SHADOW

SHAPE

SHARPENING

SIZE

SLICE

SNAPSHOT

SPOT CHANNEL

INDEX

U

UNDOING

V

VIEW

W

WARPING

WEB

See also PHOTO GALLERY

WORKSCREEN

Z

ZOOM